Driftwood Furniture

Driftwood Furniture

Practical Projects

for Your Home and Garden

Derek Douglas

FIREFLY BOOKS

A Firefly Book

Published by Firefly Books Ltd. 2003

First printing

Publisher Cataloging-in-Publication Data (U.S.)
(Library of Congress Standards)
Douglas, Derek.
  Driftwood furniture : practical projects for your home and garden/ Derek Douglas –1st ed.
[144] p. : ill., photos. (some col.) ; cm.
Includes index.
Summary: Guide to constructing 19 driftwood items including furniture and decorative objects.
ISBN 1-55297-729-3
ISBN 1-55297-702-1 (pbk.)
1. Furniture making—Amateurs' manuals. 2. Woodwork—Amateurs' manuals. 3. Driftwood. I. Title.
684.1/04 21 TT185.D67 2003

Published in the United States in 2003 by
Firefly Books (U.S.) Inc.
P.O. Box 1338, Ellicott Station
Buffalo, New York 14205

Printed in Canada by Friesens, Altona, Manitoba

Editor: Anna Filippone
Design and layout: Tinge Design Studio
Illustrator: Kara Bunn

National Library of Canada Cataloguing in Publication Data
Douglas, Derek, 1933-
  Driftwood furniture : practical projects for your home and garden / Derek Douglas.
Includes index.
ISBN 1-55297-729-3 (bound).—
ISBN 1-55297-702-1 (pbk.)
  1. Rustic woodwork—Amateurs' manuals. 2. Furniture making—Amateurs' manuals. 3. Garden ornaments and furniture—Design and construction—Amateurs' manuals. 4. Garden structures—Design and construction—Amateurs' manuals. 5. Driftwood. I. Title.
TT180.D69 2003   684.1'04   C2003-902810-0

Published in Canada in 2003 by
Firefly Books Ltd.
3680 Victoria Park Avenue
Toronto, Ontario, M2H 3K1

The Publisher acknowledges the financial support of the Government of Canada through the Book Publishing Industry Development Program for its publishing activities.

Dedication

This book is dedicated to my father and to my mother for the values and Irish humor they instilled in all 12 of us. My mother remains in my memory as a saint. Anyone that mothered 12 children through the 20s, 30s and 40s had to be.

Acknowledgment

There have been a lot of people who have helped and encouraged me in my endeavors – too many to mention individually – but I would like to give a special thank you to Marina owner Dick Peever for all his help and encouragement. Without it, this book would not have been completed.

Table of Contents

Chapter 5

Chapter 6

Introduction

I love a storm …

I'm not talking about the kind of storm described in Sebastian Junger's *The Perfect Storm*, with hundred-foot waves and terrifying intensity. No, the storms I love are the ones that Mother Nature throws at us now and again that find all the trees – trees that have had their roots undermined by heavy rains or have been felled by beavers. Mother Nature sweeps up all the debris with wind and rain into the world's largest washing machine: the lakes and oceans. She debarks the trees, removes branches, thoroughly cleans them, then tumbles them around for weeks, even years. At long last, with the arrival of the storm, they're pounded onto beaches for the final bleach-and-dry cycle.

That's where I come in. Almost five years ago, as I walked along the boardwalk of my favorite town, Goderich, Ontario, I found my first piece of driftwood. It was silvery white, with a finish smoother than sandpaper could produce, so hard it was almost petrified and had such an interesting shape that my imagination was instantly ignited.

Since then, hundreds of trips to the beach have allowed me to create garden furniture and sculptures that are strong, artistically appealing in a rustic way and will last for years to come. Mother Nature is ruthless about determining what pieces survive that pounding on the rocks and beaches – the survivors dull my tools with their incredible hardness and make assembly a little more challenging. The result is well worth the effort.

One thing I have learned after traversing the beaches for the last few years is that it becomes obvious that whatever sinks out there in the lakes and oceans invariably ends up on our beaches – albeit in pieces. On our local beach I have come across parts of vessels that sank or were scuttled a hundred years ago. I've seen log beams 12-by-12-inches square with long 1½-inch spikes through them.

During one particularly heavy storm last summer, there was a tornado warning. The result was a 5-foot rise in the water level of the Maitland River beside us. The floating debris that passed us the next day consisted of an assortment of driftwood logs, two picnic tables, a small overturned boat, dock remnants and an incredible amount of silt. All this material was swept out a mile or so into the lake, then picked up by the onshore waves and dumped onto the lovely sandy beach.

The best time to find ample driftwood on the beach is following a storm.

It was quite an eyesore. The beach had been so pristine and picturesque, but after the storm there was this band of tangled mess that stretched for miles along the shoreline. Now there was a race against time to retrieve some pieces of this driftwood before the "firebugs" got to it. In their haste to clean up the beach, town workers pile up the debris and burn it. Unfortunately, all the burnable pieces are usually those that are easily carried and, of course, are the nicest and most suited to my hobby. That day, though, I was quicker than they were and found some great pieces to add to my collection.

I hope to instill the enthusiasm I have for building driftwood furniture to my readers because, believe me, the satisfaction of finding your first pieces, putting your imagination in gear and making your first creation cannot be described. You will, I'm sure, catch the fever that I've experienced and will want to press on to your next project, and the one after that, and the one after that....

This book's purpose is to introduce you to a hobby that is not only absorbing and exciting, but the end result is that you wind up with some useful, long-lasting creations that you will enjoy along with everyone else. I have grown a passion for driftwood that borders on obsession. No, *addiction* is more the word. I can't resist the call to the beach, especially following a storm. I store the driftwood knowing that if I don't, someone will get to it first and burn it on a beach campfire.

On the following pages, you will find many ideas, information on ways to get started, production tips and detailed instructions for 19 driftwood projects. Great lengths have been taken to document the progress of some of the projects. Difficulty levels vary from nice and easy, right up to challenging and intricate.

This hobby can be enjoyed by the whole family or by any individual person. It is very economical, stimulating to the imagination and a thoroughly healthy outdoor pastime. The health benefits include the many walks along the beaches and river edges, the fresh air you get from working outside and the muscular activity required to achieve your results. I also think that the complete absorption of your mind while it's wrapped up in the creative process relieves you from the everyday stresses of world news, stock market fluctuations, housework, the kids' problems and so on.

It is true that you need somewhere to work and a bench. My workbench is my picnic table at the cottage, but you can scale down the size of any project to fit your available working quarters. The sun may be a factor to contend with if you work outside – I had to buy a 9-foot umbrella to protect my fair skin. The tools required are covered in Chapter 3, but bear in mind that you can get away with just a few to start and as you get more ambitious you can expand your arsenal later.

If you live alongside or near a lake or river shoreline, then you are very fortunate and can begin almost immediately. Others will need to venture out when they can to find the pieces they need. Although I stress the source of wood to be off the beaches and rivers, I find that woodlots can also be loaded with interesting pieces. Weathered wood obtained from lightning-struck trees or those that have succumbed to rot invariably take others down with them, thereby making for some excellent supplies.

I believe this hobby provides one of the most unfettered ways of building furniture for your home or garden. You have complete freedom to continually change your design (remember, almost everything is screwed or bolted together to enable you to do this) right up to the finish. You don't have to worry about scratching any pieces, varnishing or painting, or even the odd hole drilled in error. Nothing can faze you in your endeavors.

It is hard to imagine that this might be the first book ever written devoted totally to this subject, but I'm sure from now on, there will be others. Building with driftwood is an entirely unique experience. And after all is said and done, there is a certain satisfaction in knowing that there is not another piece in the world quite the same as yours.

Have fun.

Fill up your trunk with all the driftwood you can find.

Chapter 1: Why Driftwood?

Why indeed? After all, there are a lot of different building materials out there. Wouldn't it be easier to go to your local lumber supplier and pick out a few lengths of two-by-four? Maybe. But if you're like me, you will come to realize that building with driftwood has certain advantages that just can't be equaled with anything else.

As I mentioned in the Introduction, Mother Nature exerts her most powerful forces – sun, air and water – on this wood to give it a resilient quality. There's no doubt about it, driftwood is good, sturdy stuff. And one of the main criteria required for a piece of furniture to last is that it has to be built to withstand years of use and abuse, otherwise it will just fall apart. As long as your joints are solid, using driftwood as your base material will ensure long-lasting furniture.

Another plus is that due to its time in what I like to call Mother Nature's "durability assembly line," driftwood is much less susceptible to insect infestation than other kinds of wood. A driftwood furniture builder featured in Daniel Mack's *Making Rustic Furniture* wrote that he'd never had any insect infestation in the 24 years he'd used driftwood because the actual drifting process drowns most of the worrisome pests.

And as for the economical nature of using driftwood, there's nothing to argue about. Other than the screws and bolts you'll need to join the few pieces together, your raw material – the driftwood – is free. Few other building materials come at so low a cost.

As well, part of the enjoyment of the driftwood building hobby is the actual task of finding your wood. Don't get me wrong, I enjoy a trip to the hardware store as much as anybody, but there is no feeling equal to visiting the beach and finding that perfect piece of driftwood to spark your imagination.

Finally, there is one advantage that driftwood has over all others – its uniqueness. There's just no comparison between a piece of two-by-four lumber (that's just like the piece next to it, and the one next to that) and a one-of-a-kind piece of driftwood, with its great silver patina, that you find on the beach. Once you've finished a project you can rest assured that even if someone else out there in the world has built a similar chair, yours is an original because there is no way that any other chair could possibly be exactly the same as the one you built with the distinct pieces you found.

Hopefully you are now convinced that driftwood is the most wonderful material to work with, because I would be lying if I said that it was ideal – with no flaws or shortcomings at all. Still, any list of the "cons" of driftwood is a short one as compared to its "pros."

One of the main assets of driftwood – its durability – is also its biggest character flaw. Yes, driftwood can be difficult to work with. I can't count how many screws and drill bits I've broken over the years.

As well, there is the potential frustration of finding the perfect piece, one that inspires you to a new project ... and having to put it aside for a while because it needs to dry out. However, this "flaw" will teach you a beneficial virtue: patience. And it sure can't hurt to have some of that when you're busy building a project you haven't tackled before, with a material you may never have used before. To quote Dan Mack:

Working with Natural Forms helps develop

tolerance and forgiveness

the appreciation of approximation

the celebration of differences

the value of deformities.

After a washout, free building materials are available at your local beach.

Chapter 2: Acquiring Driftwood

It may seem obvious, but one of the first things you will need to do is gather the driftwood you'll be using in your projects. You will also need to store the wood you find. I've learned a few things over the past few years that you may find helpful with regards to collecting, selecting and storing your driftwood.

Insects

Although it rarely happens, the wood you collect could have bug infestations and should be treated if such is the case. This is particularly important if the piece is going to end up in your house. Mother Nature sees to it that she debugs wood in her "washing machine," but nevertheless keep an eye out for pieces that have pinholes or tunnels, as you could have problems. Also, if you collect pieces that are wet and they stay wet, termites or earwigs could decide to move in. If you have a questionable piece, isolate it from the rest of your wood and test it by making a cut or two to see if there are any insects. If so, get rid of it.

Collecting

The main rule to keep in mind when collecting driftwood is to avoid trespassing. Ever been turfed off a beach? I have. It is not a pleasant experience. Be aware of how you access and depart from the beach. Always look for the "public access" points. Keep track of where you are going and be respectful. If you happen to wander too far into private frontage, don't take a shortcut through someone's lane. Retrace your steps. To keep it simple: *If in doubt, stay out.* Facing a Doberman can be a nervy experience.

Another thing to keep in mind – and this one may be hard to grasp – is that sometimes you just don't need to get more driftwood. Yes, initially you will want to go to the beach a lot, to build up your supplies and have a good selection. You will reach a point, though, when you're just putting things off – avoiding a project, maybe. That, or else you find you enjoy the *collecting* process more than the *building* process. So once in a while, just build from what you already have and don't go collecting.

Selecting

I'm often asked if I look for a piece of driftwood to make a particular project or do I get inspired by the shape or character of a piece that I find. For me, it's a bit of both. I therefore tell people to just pick up whatever they can, based on their space and needs, and think about it later. Some pieces jump out at you to go into a project.

Only use solid wood pieces that are free of decay and are hardwood (usually quite heavy). If in doubt, bang the piece in question against a rock or another large log. If it has a dull sound, don't use it for crucial framework. If it is a nice piece with lots of character, by all means keep it for later use (that is, for filler pieces where it wouldn't take much stress). If you find a character-rich piece that has some rot, it doesn't necessarily have to be passed over. If you can cut or carve out the rotted section and still get a sound piece, by all means take it.

Initially, if you are new to the experience, you will probably be overenthusiastic and pick up everything in sight. This is not necessarily a bad thing. You'll soon get the hang of what you want to take and what you don't.

When you get more established and you have built a few projects, it will be important to remember to replenish your stock. Even if you're itching to get to the beach after a storm, take a moment to check your woodpile. Are you getting low on big, long pieces? How's your stock of curved wood looking? Knowing what you need might also help you prepare for your beachcombing trip. After all, there is no use in giving your husband or wife the pickup truck for the day if you are planning on going off to find 10-foot lengths of wood.

Always keep an eye out for the less common finds. Y-shaped pieces or ones with good, gnarled roots should always be picked up because you never know when you'll find a similar piece again.

Finally, although the focus in this book is on driftwood, don't overlook wood that hasn't been found on or near water. Feel free to take a little "artistic license." Weathered wood – that is, wood that has been exposed to the elements – can still have the right patina to "match" with your driftwood. Don't overlook items you might find tossed out, in an old woodpile or at garage sales, like old crates, a collapsed barn or shed, doors, and so on. I've used other types of weathered wood in some of my projects to great effect.

Picking and Choosing

Is this piece of driftwood really worth taking? If your space is limited, or you just don't want to end up collecting a lot of "junk," ask yourself this question before you load up every inch of wood you can find. If in doubt, do a quick evaluation based on the following:

- Is the piece free of decay?
- Is it good hardwood?
- Are you lacking this kind of piece in your woodpile?
- Can you physically transport this piece?
- Is it a very unique piece you might never find again?

My neighbor Wendy carries a long piece of driftwood. I try to avoid cutting such pieces down in size until I decide on a suitable project.

Decorative Root Pieces

As attractive as they are, they can't always be relied upon for areas that need strengthening. However, they can transform an otherwise dull design into a much more interesting piece.

Transporting

Carrying the heavy pieces along the beach for sometimes up to a mile can be very tiring, hard work, especially on those hot, humid summer days when there isn't a breath of wind. One such day my wife and I were struggling with two very desirable, long and heavy pieces with the roots still attached. Out of the blue, my wife said, "Why don't we try floating them along?" Brilliant. That's right, she's not just a pretty face.

Feet bared, we pulled and pushed these gems for over a half a mile to where the car was parked. Halfway back I had to put my running shoes back on to protect my feet and now each waterlogged shoe felt like it weighed 20 pounds. Then, when we tried to lift the logs out, they had almost doubled their weight thanks to the water. What a job we had to lug them over the dunes! Not recommended. Oh well, my wife still has a pretty face.

Sorting and storing

As you begin collecting your driftwood, it is a good idea to start sorting the pieces right away into categories like the following:

- Straight, over 2½ feet long (you will find some as much as 20 to 30 feet long; I try not to cut them unless I absolutely have to)
- Curved, over 2½ feet long
- Straight, 1 to 2½ feet long
- Curved, 1 to 2½ feet long
- Short lengths, under 1 foot long
- Small pieces, ¾ to 1½ inches in diameter
- Root and other unusually shaped pieces (good for bracing)
- Y-shaped pieces, all sizes

If you stop to take the time to sort your pieces you will be amazed how it speeds up the construction process. It is also well worth the extra space it will take up. There is nothing more frustrating than trying to look through a woodpile that is nothing more than a tangled mess and keep turning the same pieces over and over again to find just the right one.

While sorting through your pieces, be sure to check them for hard-to-see or hidden nails and screws, as these will ruin most cutting tools. Also watch out for fishing hooks, especially in root pieces. Remove these unwanted tidbits before storing your pieces away so you don't have to have the added job when you start constructing.

Cleaning and drying

Mother Nature will have taken care of some of your driftwood by having cleaned, bleached and dried it before it ends up in your hands. It is likely that you are going to have to do some work on some of the wood before you can store it away.

You can get rid of silt, sand and salt by washing the wood off with some mild soapy water and scrubbing it with a good wire brush. If there's any bark or

My wife, Shirley, makes transporting driftwood easier with this golf cart.

grunge imbedded in the wood that you don't like, it may require sanding.

Waterlogged wood will need to be dried out — a process that could take a few months. Find a dry, well-ventilated place and spread out the wood, or use a drying rack. And remember, patience is a virtue. Don't rush the process by drying the wood near a fire or else it could crack or split. Also, if the wood is very wet, you'll want to turn it periodically so you don't get mildew stains.

Tree Species

You probably won't care too much about the type of wood you collect as long as it is strong, safe and suitable for the project at hand. You will likely collect some or all of the following species: ash, beech, birch, cedar, chestnut, elm, fir, locust, maple, oak, pine, spruce and walnut. For further details, such as hardness, toughness, decay resistance and the odor rating of these species. I would refer you to Drew Langsner's very interesting and informative book Green Woodworking. Mr. Langsner also gives a good coverage of why wood rots and methods to prevent such decay.

Safe beachcombing

Many people know the basic workshop safety tips, but there are also safety issues to keep in mind when you're out beachcombing.

- Be careful when collecting driftwood on some beaches. The best pieces can be in very hard-to-reach places. If you happen to be at a rocky beach, watch for those surfaces that are wet or especially weedy, as these are really dangerous. I took a nasty fall on one such rock but, fortunately, when I fell, my chest landed on a flat rock and I was only winded for a few minutes.
- Always let someone know which beach you're going to. After I took that fall I just mentioned, I realized that I could not be seen from the shore and it made me think of just how dangerous the situation could have been if no one knew where I was.
- Watch where you're going. I was running along the beach on one occasion because the load I was carrying was becoming heavier and more cumbersome with each step. Suddenly I was chewing sand. I had tripped on some protruding thin wire I hadn't been able to see. Fortunately, my headlong lunge left me with no more than hurt pride.
- Keep an eye on your surroundings. Another time, I was carrying a 10-foot piece of wood on my shoulder and walking against a really strong wind. My hearing is not the best and what with this howling wind as well, I didn't know that there were three kids on small screaming dirt bikes coming up behind me until the first one zoomed by. I nearly jumped out of my skin. It was lucky for the other two that I didn't turn around because my log would have taken them both off their bikes, Charlie Chaplin-style.
- Don't carry too much at one time. Better still, if you're on the hunt for big pieces, bring someone with you to share the load.
- Wear a hat on sunny days. It's easy to forget how nasty a sunburn can be when your thoughts are occupied with driftwood hunting.
- If there's a big pile of debris, use a long stick to poke at it before plunging your arm in. You never know if something sharp has washed up on shore or if some unseen animal is lurking.
- Finally, be careful if you're driving on sand, especially if you're not used to it or don't have the right vehicle for it. You could get stuck.

Chapter 3: Tools and Materials

This is a hobby that can be enjoyed with a varied list of tools, depending on your physical strength, age, stamina and pocketbook. For example, a jigsaw and handsaw could be used instead of a bandsaw, but the physical effort is much more strenuous. Try it for a day. I'm sure you will agree.

When I first started on this newfound hobby, I was 64 years young and in reasonably good health. Years later I find that my stamina just "ain't what it used to be." For your guidance, then, I will list the tools that I use. Many of them are a must if you are going to get into this seriously. However, you can customize your own list and add to your arsenal as you go along.

Money-Saving Tips

Although this already is an economical hobby, there are still ways to cut costs.
- Buy your lag bolts and screws in bulk. You can save up to 60 percent on the cost.
- Saw blades can also be bought in bulk. I buy my blades six at a time for economy.

Cutting tools

As it happens when you're working with natural or found materials, they likely won't be the right shape or length that you need, so you'll have to cut them to size. You may also have to make some notches. I use the following tools when doing driftwood work.

- Portable bandsaw – This sits on your workbench and can be clamped in place. I use a ⅜-inch blade because a ¼-inch tends to wander too much. There are times when I wished I had bought the next model up.
- Handsaw – This tool is always kept in my car trunk. Mine is a Swedish one called a Barracuda, and if you feel the teeth you'll know why. It is vicious and will slice through an 8-inch log in minutes. Keep your fingers out of the way of this one.
- Jigsaw – This is a really handy tool for notches that are sometimes very difficult to do with the bandsaw. I buy the longest blades that I can and use six teeth per inch. This is a "must have" tool.

Drilling tools

To make solid joints, you're going to be connecting 99 percent of your pieces together with screws and lag bolts, and predrilling everything. I recommend having two different drills. Both should be variable-speed types, one for drilling holes and the other for screwing (Robertson or Phillips bit). It's always helpful to have a good set of drill bits – up to ⅜-inch.

Sanding and shaping tools

You'll need these for finishing work since you won't want to get caught, scraped or snagged on any of the furniture you're building. The following is what I use, though you don't need them all for the work you'll be doing.

- End sander – This is a tremendous labor-saving device. My Dremel has a 5-inch disc and sanding discs held on with Velcro. I generally use a 60-grit, but other grits are available.
- Sanding drum – What you're looking for is the type that can occasionally fit in your drill. The diameter should be 2 to 3 inches so you can occasionally use it to make some notches instead of using your jigsaw or bandsaw. Use whichever is easiest for the task at hand.

- Dremel drill – I use this tool for shaping the gripping handle of my wheelbarrows, using a 1¼-inch mushroom compound curve attachment from Dura-Grit. You could also use a round-shaped Micro Plane.
- Belt sander – This is a handheld sander. It is not an essential item, but if you have one already it is useful for leveling the seat and back pieces that cause discomfort.

Other tools and materials

There are a few other items you should keep handy.

- Socket wrench – This is for securing your lag bolts. It should be for ¼-inch size bolts.
- Hammer – Although all the projects are assembled using screws and lag bolts, a hammer is still useful to have around on those occasions when a broken screw juts out of a piece and you just can't get it out. If all else fails, you can use your hammer to just bang the screw into the wood.
- Sanding blocks and sandpaper – Periodically, you have to hand-sand a piece. A couple of blocks are enough – one a 60-grit and the other a 120-grit.
- Clamps – You'll generally need a few medium-sized ones.
- Tape measure – A 12-footer will be sufficient.
- Glue gun – This is really only necessary if you are going to be making smaller scale projects.
- Extension cord – Be sure it's a heavy-duty one with an overload fuse.
- Screws – Use the brass-colored type in #8 size in 1¼-inch, 2-inch, 2½-inch and 3-inch. Buy lots in bulk. You should also have a few #10 3½-inch.
- Lag bolts – You'll need a variety of sizes: 3-inch, 3½-inch, 4-inch, 4½-inch and 5-inch. Again, buy in quantity unless you are sticking with small-scale projects.

Workshop safety

There are a variety of safety rules to keep in mind when you're working.
- Always wear safety glasses.
- Have a first-aid kit on hand, with gauze, bandages and ointment.
- Protect your hearing by wearing earplugs whenever you use loud machinery.
- Know your tools and respect them. Anything mechanically driven has the potential to harm.
- Unplug tools if you are working on them, for example, when changing a saw blade.
- Keep your shirttails tucked in, roll up your sleeves, remove any jewelry and make sure your shoelaces are tied. You don't want to trip or get anything fed into a "hungry" machine.
- Pull out extension cord plugs if you have to leave your work. Kids can be curious.
- Keep youngsters well back if they want to watch you work.

- Secure work properly for difficult cuts. Use clamps or have someone hold the piece down.
- Keep both hands back of the sharp end of your chisel if you have to use one.
- Don't work in the rain.
- Work in good lighting.
- Keep your working area clean and uncluttered.

The #1 Safety Tip

The list of potential safety tips could be endless. The main rule to remember? Don't take unnecessary risks.

My neighbor Elaine shows that a wheelbarrow is just one of many attractive items you can build.

You will find that mirror-cutting is useful for a variety of projects.

- Arms for chairs and benches
- Patterned backrests of chairs and benches
- Decorative bracing for bench fronts and chairs
- Trellises
- Arbors
- Sleighs

Chapter 4: Working with Driftwood

It isn't difficult to master the techniques needed to work with driftwood. I've outlined everything you'll need to know to be confident in building your first project.

Mirror-cutting

My greatest discovery since I picked up my first piece of driftwood was mirror-image cutting. It all came about when I was having trouble finding two matching arms for the bench I'd been planning on building.

There was a particularly lovely piece of wood in my pile – it had a well-shaped curve and a distinctive, worn, root-shaped end; however, it was a tad too big. Then the idea struck me: Why not try to cut it down the middle? Once I split it, I would end up with a nicely splayed-out look on either side of the bench. As an added benefit, the flat surface created by the saw cut would make for a more comfortable armrest and provide a good, level surface to set a drink on, too.

Unfortunately, it was too thick and hard for my little bandsaw. So I did a local check around for someone who had a larger bandsaw than I did, and I was referred to Bill Kelly, a quiet unassuming man who is a complete wood craftsman. He has built everything from houses to reproduction grandfather clocks.

Bill is retired, but he still puts in a full day in his workshop. He has cut many, many pieces for me since I first met him. Sometimes it has meant changing the blade in his two-horsepower bandsaw – a half-hour job for sure. I hope everyone is as fortunate as I am and can find a "Bill Kelly" near them.

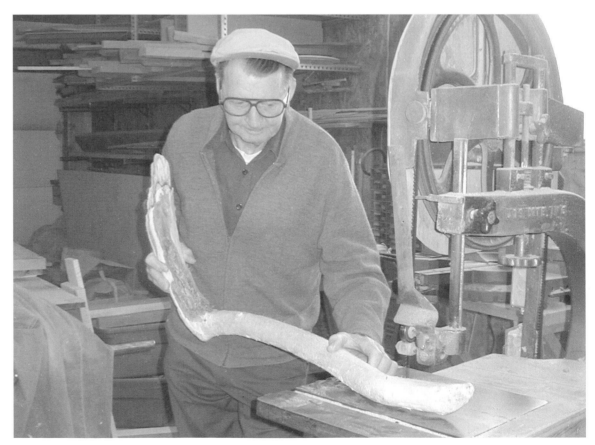

Bill Kelly demonstrates how to mirror-cut driftwood.

Mirror-cutting opened up whole new avenues for my designs, and as you will see in some of the photographs and sketches that follow, I have incorporated them into many of my driftwood pieces.

I have one warning, however: Once cut, some pieces will warp. Warping mainly occurs when the wood is not fully dried. After the piece is cut, the forces of tension within it are released and the shape becomes somewhat distorted. Don't despair, though. Those same warped pieces can come into use on a later project. It's happened to me with some surprising and pleasing results. So if your pieces warp, just set them aside for another task, and look for some new pieces for the project you're working on.

Joinery

I join almost everything with screws (#8 and #10) and lag bolts (¼-inch). All holes are predrilled for this purpose. This, I believe, is a must. The main drawback of using nails is that they are hard to remove if you want to rearrange pieces of wood. And by predrilling, you'll avoid splitting the wood.

Using screws and lag bolts makes assembly design changes easier; it also strengthens your project and therefore will make it safer. Another plus: should a part break some time in the future, it is much easier to replace.

However, on some of my smaller pieces, I find that wiring them together is more practical. I've used both copper wire and steel wire on bird feeders with considerable success.

Instead of making this hobby look too complicated, I believe in the KISS approach. We will not be calling for mortise and tenons, and dovetails or even blind dovetails. I have illustrated here all the joints that you will ever need to make any project in this book.

The simplest type of joint will only require simple bolting of one piece to another, as in the image, below left. However, this creates a weak joint. By simply notching one of the pieces to fit the other, a much stronger joint is made (below right).

Broken Bits

Broken drill bits and screws are going to become a more regular part of your life. The solution is simple. If the broken piece is sticking out just a small amount – enough to get a hold of it with a vice grip – then you will be able to easily twist it out. If not, then just take your trusty hammer and bang the broken end into the wood and drill another hole next to it. There, isn't driftwood furniture building a forgiving hobby?

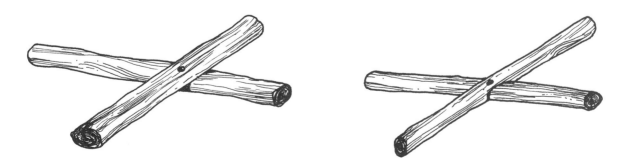

Use notches whenever a more secure fit is required. Depending on how the pieces will connect, you will need to create either round or square notches, using your bandsaw or jigsaw.

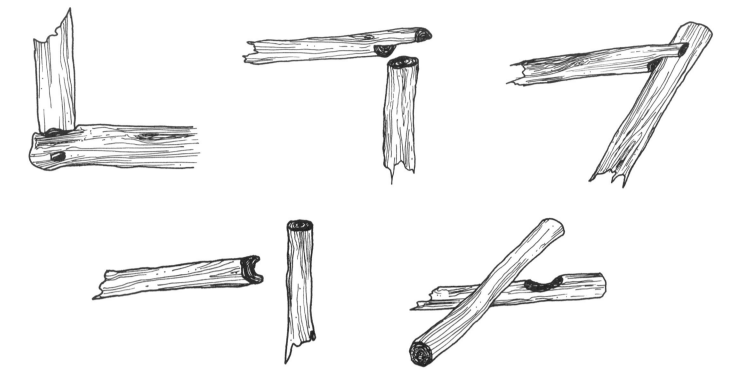

I particularly enjoy working with Y-shaped pieces because they already have a natural "notch" in place. Occasionally, though, even Y-shaped pieces will need a little shaping to snugly connect with another piece.

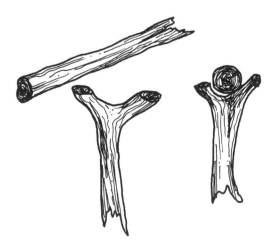

Bracing

Always brace your creations sufficiently. Whether it is a bench, an arbor or a wheelbarrow, any of your constructions can be subject to a lot of abuse from people and weather. They should be absolutely solid. Mother Nature would like it that way.

Study the following diagrams of bracing because they are very important to any project that you undertake and will serve you well.

In general, you will need to brace any stress points on the piece of furniture you are building. Corners frequently require bracing to provide support for joints, and sometimes to keep a project square. You can use straight, curved or even Y-shaped pieces as bracing.

It is very important to have enough bracing on any piece of furniture that will support weight – particularly those pieces of furniture that support the weight of people, like benches, loveseats and chairs. Always brace all joints in chair and bench backs.

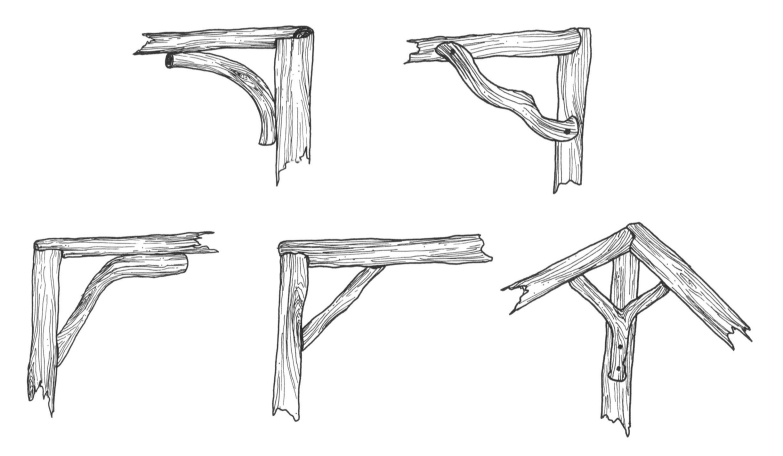

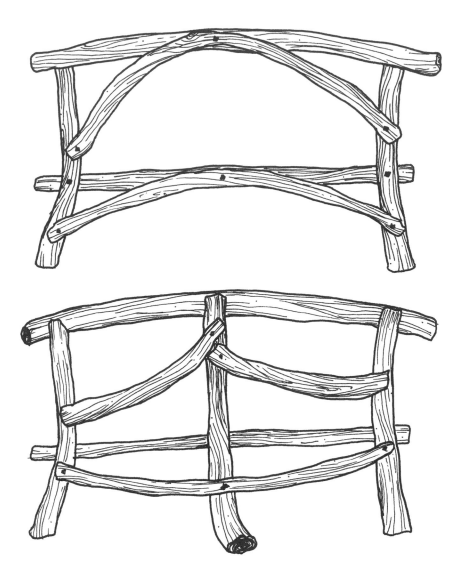

Furniture legs take much of the brunt of a person's weight, so ensure they are also well braced. Cross-braces are particularly useful on chair legs, and look attractive, too.

Drilling

When drilling two pieces of wood that will be joined by lag bolts, always drill a hole in the first piece large enough so that the lag bolt will push through by hand. The second piece will have a smaller hole. Doing this will ensure that the two pieces will pull together securely. If you drill both pieces with small holes, they will never pull tightly together.

Make sure that the holes you drill for lag bolts are deep enough. The wood can be so hard that you will break off the top of the lag bolt, even if you are only short by a little. Believe me, correcting it is time-consuming and frustrating.

If you decide to countersink the head of a lag bolt, on the arm of a bench for instance, start by drilling a hole big enough to fit the head of the lag bolt plus the socket wrench that you will be using on it. Drill this hole just deep enough to accommodate the thickness of the bolt cap. Then you will drill the next stage of the hole as usual. You should be able to push the bolt through with your finger and check that the head cannot be felt when you slide your hand over the spot.

Sanding and finishing

Always sand off the stubs of branches that you have removed. They invariably get in the way at some crucial joint. It looks better too.

Using sandpaper doesn't require much skill, but you do need to be patient and sustained in your effort. If there are small spaces that need some sanding, tear the sandpaper into long, thin strips and pull the strip back and forth around curves, through holes, and so on.

I'm always asked if some sort of finish should be put on the wood. At this point in time I say no. I once put some boiled linseed oil on one of my chairs and was disappointed when I saw the results. My good neighbor had one of those power washers that he uses to wash his cedar deck. He tried it on the chair and could not bring it back to its original patina.

My three-year-old benches look as good as when I first put them together. The wood has endured all the hardships Mother Nature has bestowed upon it. Therefore, I find "au natural" is the best.

I did try staining a piece of driftwood and asked friends whether they thought that it would improve the looks of the project that I was working on. They all said that they preferred the natural gray look.

Wheels

While on your daily travels, keep an eye out for any iron wheels you can use for your projects. I've discovered wheels in all kinds of places: barns, flea markets, farmyards, antique shops and garage sales. Then I discovered pulleys – the "second cousin" of the wheel – that were sometimes even nicer in design than the regular wheel.

Chapter 5: Building Driftwood Furniture

If you have read what's been written so far, you will have a good idea of the nature of driftwood, how to work with it, what tools and materials you will need and what to expect. If you have not read anything yet, don't build anything! Save yourself from some frustrating experiences by at least reading the last chapter, Working with Driftwood. You don't want to make some of the mistakes I have, believe me.

To further prepare you in your driftwood adventure, the following photo essay follows through the assembly of a driftwood bench.

Building a garden bench

Figure 1

My friend Larry Lee has already gathered all the materials needed for this project (see Fig. 1). His tools are within reach, and he has piled up all the driftwood pieces he will need for the bench, as indicated in the material list. (Lists of required materials and tools are provided with each outlined project in this book.) He first lays out the pieces for the back of the bench. Holes for lag bolts are predrilled and the frame for the back of the bench is then assembled.

The next step is to attach the seat rails and front legs (see Fig. 2). At this stage it can be tricky to keep pieces in place while you are working on them. If you don't have an able body around to help, you can always lean pieces against a picnic table or workbench. Or you can prop them up as Larry has here. To complete the basic frame of the bench, Larry attaches the arms (see Fig. 3).

Figure 2

With the frame assembled, this is a good time to take a step back and see how everything looks. Also stop to check on how stable and level the bench is. At this point, it isn't braced, so

Figure 3

it doesn't need to be rock-solid, but ensure all the joints are secure and that the bench isn't wobbly.

Larry lays out the seat pieces before securing them in place (see Fig. 4). Rough edges will be hand-sanded so the seat is more comfortable and clothing can't snag. Notice how Larry has already laid out pieces for the back of the bench, ready for the next step.

Larry attaches one of the back supports. This photo (see Fig. 5) provides a good view of the back leg with its Y-shaped top. This type of natural notch is one of the unique features of working with driftwood as a building material.

Nearly done. The last task is to complete the back of the bench (see Fig. 6). Once fully assembled, it's time to take a seat on the bench and see how it feels. Sand any rough edges you missed. Add bracing, if necessary.

Figure 4

Figure 5

Figure 6

The finished bench

Developing your own projects

While there is a wide sampling of projects to work on in the next chapter, you may nevertheless want to develop your own designs and build your own pièce de résistance. I would suggest you try your hand at a few of the outlined projects before moving on to your own designs. By doing so, you will keep things a little simpler and more relaxing for yourself while you get used to building with driftwood.

Remember, there are few rules to this hobby. Just ensure that your project is strong and safe, attractive to the eye and, in the case of furniture you might sit on, smooth and comfortable.

Coming up with ideas

Sometimes an idea just hits you. Other times you might find a piece of driftwood, and its shape is what inspires you to build a particular piece. Or maybe what you're building comes out of necessity; for example, you could really use some chairs and a table in your yard. However, sometimes it's not that simple.

One way to get ideas for a project is to look at your interests. Do you enjoy reading? If so, why not fashion a magazine rack. Do you like making things for your children or grandchildren? Then consider building a miniature set of tables and chairs.

Magazines or books also contain a multitude of ideas. Just keep an open mind. Remember, a dining room table doesn't have to be made of solid cherry. If you're looking for something a little different, maybe the enormous mass of tangled driftwood roots you found last week could be sanded smooth and topped with a round piece of glass to make a very different kind of table that would be a much better conversation piece than something you bought at Sears for a lot of money. When it comes to options for driftwood, the possibilities are almost endless.

Possible projects

Still stuck for ideas? Okay, I'll let you off the hook. Here are just a handful of ideas for things you can build out of driftwood.

- bridge
- child-sized furniture
- coffee table
- doll cradle
- drying stand
  (for wet boots and mittens)
- end table
- footstool
- gate
- gazebo

- hat rack
- ladder
- loveseat
- magazine rack
- mirror frame
- picnic table
- picture frame
- stool
- table base

Miniatures

One time last year, I was asked to make one of my creations again, but this time on a miniature scale. I did it, but never again. It took almost as long to put together as the full-sized one. I changed to #6 size screws but now I realize that I should have used my trusty glue gun. This would have eliminated all the screwing and drilling and looked better.

Often it's the unique shape of a piece that inspires a new design.

Typical furniture dimensions

To help you fine-tune some of the details, the following are fairly standard dimensions for some of the more common types of furniture. However, always remember that you can always take a little artistic license and follow your own rules. I certainly have.

Furniture type	Dimensions
Dining table	Height: 29" to 30" Allow a minimum 24" per person; ideally it should be 30"
Coffee table	Height: 12" to 18"
End table	Height: 18" to 24"
Chair	Seat height: 15" to 18" Seat width: 17" to 20" Seat depth: 15" to 18" Arms: 8" to 10" higher than seat
Sofa or loveseat	Seat height: 14" to 17" Seat width: minimum 24" per person Seat depth: 15" to 18"
Nightstand	Arms: 8" to 10" higher than seat Height: 18" to 22"

The project plan

You have an idea of what you're going to build. That's the first step in creating a project plan. However, before you start building you have a bit of work to do. Namely, you have to take that flimsy idea and put it down on paper. You have to take the concept and give it real measurements, then determine what materials you need, and in what order you are going to put them together.

This might seem like a lot of work, but don't skip this step. If you take the time to plan things out ahead of time you will save yourself a lot of aggravation later. Yes, building driftwood furniture is likely to just be a hobby for you, something you do with your spare time, but why spend your spare time feeling frazzled? You will find this hobby a lot more relaxing if it doesn't frustrate you!

Hopefully you have taken the time to build a few projects outlined in the book. It's a good idea to have experience with building with driftwood on an outlined project rather than just going willy-nilly off on your own. Not that you can't – as I've said, there are few rules to this hobby – but it can't hurt to have a little foreknowledge.

If you have reviewed the how-to projects, you might have noticed there was a kind of template in place for each one. If you include all the parts of the planning process used in the how-to's in your own project, you have a much better chance of ending up with a good piece of furniture than if you just start screwing pieces together in the hopes it will turn out all right.

Very simply, if you spend the proper amount of time in planning out your project *before* you start building, you'll find that the project will proceed more smoothly and you'll spot potential errors before you actually make them.

If you've already done a lot of building, the planning process is likely old hat. However, I'm going to run through the basics anyway. It's good information for those who are new at this and may even provide some tips to those of you who have been building things for a while.

At first, the process might seem a bit awkward, but you'll become far more familiar with it over time and you will be happier with your results. The project plan for any piece you want to build should include the following elements.

Sketches and final drawings

It's always a good idea to start with a sketch of your idea first. This will help you to visualize and improve your project at the easiest time. Do a few sketches if necessary and maybe even build up a few ideas for future projects in a binder or notebook. I keep two binders, one in my car and one in my coffee table drawer. Putting your ideas down on paper when they occur to you will pay off. I've lost a few good ideas for not doing this at my creative moments (sometimes at 3 a.m.).

Don't worry about being an artist. These drawings don't have to be fancy or even to scale. They are simply guidelines to your projects and will only serve to help you build the project with fewer headaches.

Once you have a rough sketch that you are happy with, it's time to move on to a more formal drawing. It's amazing how different an idea of yours can look once it's actually drawn on paper. In your mind you have this perfect image of what a chair should look like, but once you sketch it, the practical side takes over. How big is the chair? How thick is each piece of wood?

Be sure to include all the specific information necessary in your drawing. That is, be sure to write in the height, width and depth of the whole piece of furniture as well as the dimensions of the individual pieces of driftwood that will make up your chair, table or whatever it is you'll be building. Then label each piece of wood needed – you can use A, B, C ... like we do in the how-to projects.

As well, you may want to make a drawing of the furniture piece from a few different views. A front view is the least of what you'll need. How should the chair look from the back? How about the sides? If you can, put all the different views on one page so you can see them all at once.

Leave your drawings aside for awhile and then have another look. Are you missing any important structural elements? Could it do with some bracing? Does anything seem out of place? It's better to find a flaw in your design before you start building.

Prototypes

I don't recommend making prototypes before building the final project – they often end up being as much work as the project itself. However, if there's a part of the construction that you're having difficulty in working out in your mind – that is, you need to see it in front of you – it might be useful to put those couple of pieces together using scrap wood.

Copying Designs

One of the best ways to build a particular piece of furniture is to find something you already like and use the same dimensions.

Materials list

Look at every piece of wood that is in your drawing. Confirm your dimensions and make a list of what you need. Check what you have on hand and make a shopping/scavenging list for what you don't have. Be specific. Note the name of the parts, their sizes (length, width and thickness), the quantities you'll need and what the piece is going to be in the final design. For example, "A" might be chair legs, so you should specify you need four of them, and they measure 4-by-4-by-24.

Don't forget about the other building materials, like lag bolts. By looking at the areas where pieces join together, you'll get a good idea of how many lag bolts and screws you'll need.

Also determine what tools you'll need to build the project. It's no use to find out halfway through your project that you really need your bandsaw, but you've lent it to your neighbor for the weekend. Finally, be sure you have any of the add-ons you need, like wheels, string, and so on.

Building sequence

Okay, you've got your drawings and you've gathered all the items on your lists. You're ready to build, right? Wrong. Before you start screwing things together, take a good, hard look at what you have and figure out where to start. Then determine what the next step is, then the next. There is a logical building order. One simple method is to combine pieces into panels or frames and then join all the panels together. If you're unsure, review the how-to projects – they will give you some ideas on how to sequence the building process.

One tip before you start building: Look at all of the pieces of wood you have selected. If some of the pieces are going to be in more prominent places, make sure they're the "nicer" pieces, with more character or a better shape. By picking through your wood ahead of time you will make a better looking piece of furniture.

While you are building

I have just one tip to remember when you are assembling your project: Keep stepping back and studying your creation as you go along and check its appearance. Is it straight? Does it look balanced? Could you improve it at this point rather than later? It is always easier to correct any errors or changes in the earlier stages of construction.

Remember that old saying "If it looks right, then it is right"? Whenever I mention this, I'm always reminded of a cartoon drawing I saw once. I can't remember where, but it showed a man standing back to study his creation – a canoe – and the canoe ends were pointed up on one end and down at the other. Oops!

This magnificent, enormous piece, full of character, disappeared or was engulfed in no time.

Chapter 6: Projects

Ready to build? Good! A variety of projects can be found on the following pages, so I'm sure that there will be at least one you will want to tackle – hopefully more. Each project is outlined with a basic plan that includes the following elements:

Materials and tools

Care has been taken to include the necessary quantities and dimensions of the driftwood needed for the project. However, it must be noted that no two pieces of driftwood are exactly alike, and that "shopping" for driftwood is not as simple as going down to the lumberyard and finding the precise dimensions you are looking for. You may have to make some substitutions or alterations on the project depending on what you have in your driftwood pile. Similarly, the list of tools provides a basic guideline to the tools you will need for the project. You may end up using different tools based on what you have in your workshop.

Choosing your wood

Although the materials list provides the basic information about the pieces of wood you'll need – that is, the quantities and measurements – the Choosing Your Wood section expands on this information by describing what part of the project the pieces are being used for, assigning a letter (A, B, C) to each part (except in the simplest of projects), as well as including further tips and suggestions on picking out particular pieces of wood. It also includes an illustration of the completed project, showing all the parts with their accompanying letter designations. However, in some instances, one or two parts of a project will not be visible in the illustration (for example, the rear pieces of a bench might not be visible in a front-view drawing); this is always noted when the parts are being described.

Building instructions

Each project includes detailed building instructions that will take you step by step through the construction process. To help you along, parts are referred to by name and letter, and illustrations are provided as a guideline. If you are already an experienced builder, you may find some of the descriptions to be simplistic; however, I have kept descriptions somewhat detailed with the novice builder in mind.

Rating

As a guideline, a difficulty rating is noted at the beginning of each project. A project labeled as a ⊤ is perfect for beginners, while a ⊤⊤⊤⊤⊤ is for expert builders.

Signpost

A welcoming project for beginners

MATERIALS		TOOLS	
8 to 10 straight pieces, 2" to 12" in diameter, 6" to 48" long	Galvanized metal strapping	Bandsaw/jigsaw	Sanding blocks
	Rope (optional)	Drill and drill bits	Screwdriver
L-shaped brackets	Decorative items, including bird feeder, wrought iron, watering cans, etc. (optional)	Handsaw	Socket wrench
Assorted screws and lag bolts			

Choosing Your Wood

While you can obviously use driftwood for this project, I've used sections from a cut-down birch tree for my signpost. (Trying to bring back logs from the beach was too much work.) Whatever your base material, you will need 8 to 10 straight pieces of various thicknesses and lengths, from 2" to 12" in diameter and 6" to 48" long.

If you do decide to use "fresh" wood, as I did, it will look nicer if all the wood is from the same species of tree. As well, make sure all bark is removed, especially if you are using birch. Birchbark holds water, so the logs will rot. My piece totally rotted away in three years.

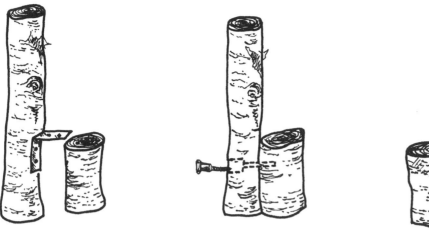

Figure 1   Figure 2   Figure 3

Building Instructions

This is one of the easiest projects in the book, and yet it is a very attractive piece to stand in front of your home or cottage. As you can see in the images, it is made up of different sized pieces of wood, of various lengths and diameters. You can follow my example in the photograph, or just use your own discretion – and artistic eye – to fit the pieces together. The real key to creating the signpost is not where to position each log, but how to secure all the pieces together.

I use three joinery methods for this project. In the first joinery method (Fig. 1), you simply connect pieces using L-shaped brackets. The brackets are screwed into each connecting piece where the top of the shorter log meets the side of the longer one.

To lag-bolt two logs together (Fig. 2), you will need to predrill holes first. Ensure that you countersink each lag bolt so it will reach well into the second log.

Finally, galvanized metal strapping can be used. See Fig. 3. Bend it around the logs and screw it in place. Don't be skimpy on the number of screws you use – you want the strapping to stay in place. Heavier logs will not need to be banded. I've also used rope in my project, but this is purely for looks and is nailed or screwed over the galvanized strapping.

I've found that you get a pleasing look if the crossbar on the top of the signpost is about the same diameter as the highest upright. To attach the crossbar, you will need to notch it first. Predrill a hole and secure with a lag bolt.

You can use the signpost as a house sign or just as a garden ornament. It can also be dressed with an old boot, watering cans, a mailbox or a bird feeder. See Fig. 4.

Figure 4

Garden Stand

A perfect resting spot for flowering plants or feathered friends

MATERIALS

A 1 curved piece, 3" to 4" in diameter, 6' to 6½' long

B 3 curved pieces, 3" to 5" in diameter, 2' to 3' long

C 1 piece of hardwood, 6" in diameter, 1" thick

D 12 curved pieces, ¾" to 1" in diameter, about 24" long

E 3 straight pieces, 1" in diameter, about 18" long

F 2 curved pieces, 1" in diameter, 12" to 15" long

Steel or copper wire

Assorted screws and lag bolts

Platforms for bird feeder or flower pots

Assorted root pieces for decoration

TOOLS

Bandsaw/jigsaw

Drill and drill bits

Needle-nose pliers

Sander

Screwdriver

Socket wrench

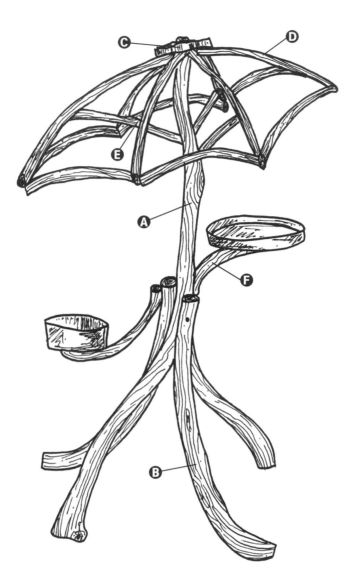

Choosing Your Wood

Ⓐ Main Upright

Sort through your woodpile for the oddest, twisted piece of wood you can find. Just make sure it's nice and thick – about 3" to 4" in diameter – and 6' to 6½' long.

Ⓑ Base Supports

As with the main upright, you're looking for odd, twisted pieces – a total of three pieces that are rich with character. Nevertheless, don't sacrifice strength for uniqueness. These base supports should be solid, strong pieces, 3" to 5" thick and 2' to 3' in length.

Ⓒ Cog-shaped Center

You'll need to use a piece of regular hardwood rather than driftwood for the cog-shaped center piece. Before you shape it, the piece will need to be about 1" thick and 6" in diameter.

❶ Umbrella

Find 12 nicely curved pieces for the umbrella. Each should be ¾" to 1" thick and roughly 24" long.

❷ Struts

These three straight pieces will be used to support the umbrella. They need to be about 1" in diameter and 18" long.

❸ Arms

Use two curved pieces for the arms, 12" to 15" long and 1" in diameter.

Building Instructions

STEP 1: Constructing the Base

This is a delightful piece to create. To start it, gather together the pieces you have chosen for your main upright (A) and base supports (B). Hopefully you've found some truly character-rich pieces – there are no better uses for them than in this project.

The main upright will be supported by the three base supports. Shape the base supports like a tripod around the main upright and use lag bolts to secure the structure in place.

Figure 1

STEP 2: Creating and Attaching the Umbrella

You can assemble the umbrella shade on your workbench. First, you will need to shape your center (C) to look like a cog. You can do this with a jigsaw or bandsaw. Drill a hole in the center of the cog-shaped piece to allow for the lag bolt that will attach the umbrella to the upright.

Next, gather your umbrella pieces (D). You will need six of them for the umbrella's ribs. I suggest you flatten these six pieces at one end using a sander, as in Fig. 1. This way, you will create a snugger fit between the ribs and the cog-shaped center piece. Screw the underside of each rib to the center piece. At this stage, your assembly should look rather spiderlike.

The other six umbrella pieces are used to connect one rib to the next at the bottom of the umbrella. Drill holes in the ends of the umbrella pieces and connect one rib to each connecting umbrella piece with wire. I generally use steel wire of a reasonable gauge rather than copper as it's stronger and cheaper. However, some people prefer the look and workability of copper.

The umbrella can now be attached to the upright. Drill a hole in the upright and secure the umbrella to it using a lag bolt. To provide extra support, you will need to attach the struts (E). They can be secured with wire or screws. If you use wire, be sure to use your needle-nose pliers to bend the wire ends over and tuck them out of the way for safety's sake.

Figure 2

STEP **3:** **Finishing Touches**

In order to put the platforms in place, you will need to attach the arms (F) first. Screw them to the upright or base supports. In my outline, I've included two arms for this project, but you can always put on more if you wish. You can use cross-sections of logs as platforms or just attach your containers directly to the arms. If you'll be using this piece as a bird feeder, be sure to drill some small holes in the bottom of the feed receptacle so rainwater won't pool inside of it.

If you like, you can add some nice root pieces between every other rib of the umbrella for a nice artistic touch, or extra platforms if need be. As well, although the structure may be solid enough as is, bracing pieces can be added to the base, as in Fig. 2.

Trellis

Give your flowering vines a place to climb

MATERIALS

A 1 Y-shaped piece, 2" to 2 ½" in diameter, 4' to 5' long

B 1 gently curved piece, 2" to 2 ½" in diameter, 4' to 5' long

C 4 slightly curved pieces, 1" to 2" in diameter, 2' to 3' long

D 2 somewhat bent pieces, 1" to 1½" in diameter, about 2' long

E 1 curved piece, 1" in diameter, 12" to 16" long

F 6 straight pieces, 2" in diameter, 8" to 10" long

G A few small pieces, 1" in diameter, 2" to 6" long

H 2 curved pieces, 1" to 2" in diameter, 3' to 4' long and 6 straight or curved pieces, 1" to 2" in diameter, 2' to 3' long

Assorted small pieces for bracing

Flat piece of wood for feeder base

Assorted screws and lag bolts

TOOLS

Bandsaw/jigsaw

Drill and drill bits

Screwdriver

Socket wrench

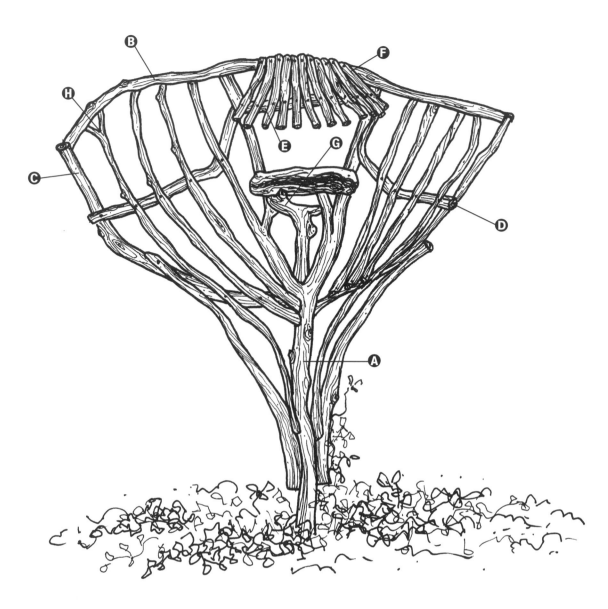

Choosing Your Wood

Ⓐ Main Support

The main support can be considered the spine of the trellis. You'll want to ensure it's a good, solid Y-shaped piece, 2" to 2½" in diameter and 4' to 5' long.

Ⓑ Upper Support

Look in your wood pile for a 2" to 2½" thick, 4' to 5' long piece that has a slight curve to it.

Ⓒ Side Supports

These pieces complete the outer frame of the trellis. Find four slightly curved pieces that are 2' to 3' long and 1" to 2" in diameter.

Ⓓ Cross Supports

To give the trellis some character, I chose cross supports that had some kinks and an unusual bend or two. This is the perfect time to use two pieces in your wood pile that are 1" to 1½" thick and about 2' long that you haven't been able to use in other projects.

❺ Roof Support

Find a simple, straight piece, 12" to 16" long and 1" in diameter.

❻ Roof

You'll require six straight pieces that are 2" in diameter and 8" to 10" long. You could also use a longer 2"-thick piece and cut it into six pieces.

❼ Feeder Base

It's good to keep small pieces of offcuts for just such a case as this. Gather together a couple of small pieces about 1" in diameter and 2" to 6" in length.

❽ Ribs

For the ribs, you'll need a total of eight straight or curved pieces that are 1" to 2" thick. Two of them should be fairly long, about 3' to 4' in length. The other six should be a variety of 2' to 3' long pieces – you'll need a couple that are fairly straight and a few others that have a bit of curve.

Building Instructions

STEP 1: Frame It

Although this is one of those kinds of projects that can just grow and build up as you go along, I've still specified all the pieces I used in mine to give you a framework to go by. You can always adjust the pieces somewhat to get a different look.

Basically, the trellis begins with a nice, fairly large Y-piece that becomes your main support (A). You can work on this project by laying the main support on the ground and attaching pieces as you go or – if your back would prefer it – assemble the pieces on a workbench or picnic table.

You'll attach the upper support (B) to the tops of the Y-shaped main support with lag bolts. Be sure to keep it centered and, if you're using a curved piece, try to find the best placement of the upper support before drilling.

To round out the frame, attach the four side supports (C) to what you've assembled. As you can see in the illustration on the opposite page, two of the pieces will attach to both the main and upper supports, while the remaining two pieces attach to the main support and the other two side supports.

Finally, bolt on the cross supports (D). Pick up the frame – it should be pretty solid.

STEP 2: The Bird Feeder

To build the feeder, we'll start with the roof and work down. Attach the roof support piece (E) to the cross supports in front of the "Y" of the main support. To create the roof pieces, you'll need to mirror-cut the 6 roof pieces (F) into 12 pieces. Screw these into place on the upper support and roof support in a slight fan shape. You may not need as many as 12 – use what's necessary.

A cross-section of a tree trunk makes a good base for the bird feeder, but you could also use any kind of flat weathered wood you have lying around. Support it with a few small pieces you've set aside for bracing. The feeder base (G) is just made by connecting a few offcuts together (see Fig. 1). Just ensure that they're all about the same diameter so you get a fairly even ledge.

STEP 3: Filling in the Gaps

To provide a little contrast, I've used both long and short ribs (H) to fill in the frame of the trellis. This pattern also helps to emphasize the bird feeder. When you're attaching the ribs, be sure to allow some space between each one so the vines that will eventually grow there have room to get through the spaces.

When you pick out the final resting place for the trellis, make sure it is well secured to the wall. When the vines envelop this it will likely become quite heavy.

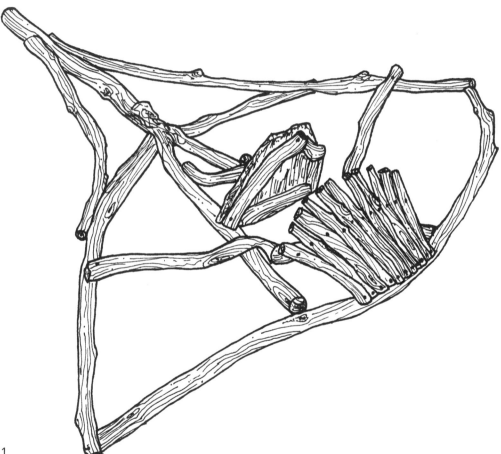

Figure 1

Four-Legged Chair

A great furniture project

MATERIALS

A 2 straight pieces, 2½" to 3½" in diameter, about 26" long

B 1 straight piece, 2" to 3" in diameter, about 24" to 26" long

C 2 straight or curved pieces, 2½" to 3½" in diameter, about 34" long

D 1 curved piece, 3" to 4" in diameter, about 24" long

E 1 curved piece, 2" to 2½" in diameter, about 24" long

F 1 straight piece, 3" to 4" in diameter, about 20" long

G 1 curved piece, 3" to 4" in diameter, about 22" long

H 5 straight pieces, 2" to 3" in diameter, about 14" to 18" long

I 3 or 4 straight pieces, 3" to 4" in diameter, about 18" long

Assorted screws and lag bolts

Assorted pieces for bracing

TOOLS

Bandsaw/jigsaw

Drill and drill bits

Sander

Screwdriver

Socket wrench

Choosing your wood

Ⓐ Front Legs

Search for two straight pieces that are 2½" to 3½" in diameter and about 26" long. Ideally, they will have a Y-shaped top, but this isn't necessary.

Ⓑ Front Seat Rail

The piece for the front seat rail should be straight and sturdy, 2" to 3" thick and about 24" to 26" long.

Ⓒ Back Legs

Look for two sturdy pieces for your back legs, 2½" to 3½" in diameter and 34" long. They can be straight or have a slight curve to them. Some kind of curve is preferable, though, because it gives the chair more stability.

Ⓓ Back Supports

You'll only need to find one piece for the two back supports – once cut down its length it'll produce the two pieces you need. Look in your driftwood pile for a nicely curved piece that's 3" to 4" in diameter and about 24" in length.

Ⓔ Rear Seat Rail (not visible)

This support piece should be nicely curved, about 24" in length and 2" to 2½" thick.

Ⓕ Side Seat Rails

As with the back supports, you're looking for a piece that you'll mirror-cut to end up with the two pieces you require. Look for a sturdy piece that's 20" in length and 3" to 4" thick.

G Arms

Once again, a mirror-cut on one piece will give you the two pieces needed here. Take care to find an interesting piece, gently curved, that's 3" to 4" in diameter and about 22" long.

H Back

For the back of your chair, you'll need to find five straight pieces that are about 14" to 18" long. You will likely need to cut them somewhat to get the right fit. The pieces can be between 2" and 3" in diameter, but try to stick with pieces that have a similar thickness to create a more even – and thus more comfortable – back for the chair.

I Seat

Look for three or four straight pieces that are about 18" long and 3" to 4" thick. Once mirror-cut, you'll have enough pieces for your seat.

Building Instructions

STEP 1: Assembling the Frame

Let's begin with the front of the chair. Find the pieces you've chosen for the front legs (A) and front seat rail (B). The rail will sit about 18" above the base of the front legs. Predrill holes and secure the front seat rail to the front legs with lag bolts.

Next we assemble the back part of the chair. Gather together the pieces for your back legs (C) and back supports (D). If you haven't mirror-cut the piece for the back support yet, there's no time like the present to get it done. Screw one of the back support pieces to the top of the back legs, flat side down. The second back support piece should be screwed to the front of the back legs about 24" from the base. See Fig. 1.

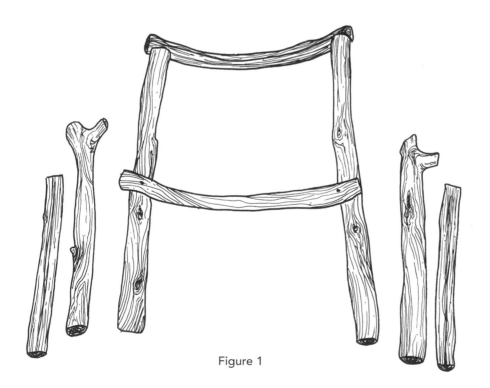

Figure 1

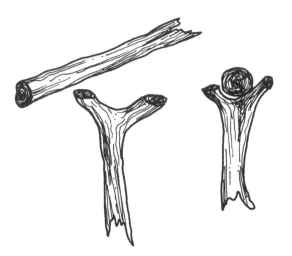

Figure 2

Since you're working on the back of the chair already, you may as well attach the rear seat rail (E). Screw it in place about 18" from the base of the back legs.

Have you noticed by now that the front of the chair is wider than the back? No, that's not a mistake. I find that making the chair this way gives it a better overall look.

To connect the front and back sections together, you'll need the two mirror-cut side seat rails (F). Screw the pieces in on top of the front and back seat rails, with the flat sides up.

Finally, to complete the basic frame of the chair, you'll put the arms (G) in place. If your front legs are equipped with a Y-shaped top, the arms can rest in the crotch of the Y. See Fig. 2. If they have a smooth end, just rest the arms on top. Either way, the arms should be placed with the flat sides up. You'll need to notch out curves at the back of the arms so they'll fit snugly to the back legs. The arms can be screwed in place at front and back or, for extra stability, lag bolts can be used to secure the arms to the back legs.

STEP 2: Bracing the Chair

Bracing should be done on all sides of the chair. The front brace should be screwed into the front legs as well

Figure 3

as the front seat rail. See Fig. 3. On the sides, two braces can be used: one that is screwed to the front and back legs and another that is connected to the side seat rail and legs.

Finally, brace the back with a piece that's screwed into each of the back legs as well as the back seat rail.

With all this bracing, your chair should feel quite solid now.

STEP 3: Fitting the Pieces for the Seat and Back

The back pieces (H) of your chair will be attached to the frame between the upper and lower back supports. I find that having the back pieces touch at the bottom and splay out at the top makes for an attractive and comfortable back rest. Make any necessary cuts to the back pieces to get them to fit and then screw them in place.

The seat pieces (I) will need mirror cuts now if you haven't done this already. Rest them flat side up on top of the front and back seat supports and screw them in place. See Fig. 4.

To finish the piece, just sand down the arms and seat. Finally, grab yourself a cool drink and sit and relax in your chair.

TIP I notched the seat pieces to create a more level sitting surface.

Figure 4

Hooded Chair

Relax and take cover from the sun

MATERIALS

A 1 straight piece, 4" to 5" in diameter, about 41" long

B 1 straight piece, 4" to 5" in diameter, about 19" long

C 1 straight piece, 4" to 5" in diameter, about 46" long

D 7 or 8 straight pieces, 2" to 2½" in diameter, about 24" long

E 2 curved pieces, 2" to 2½" in diameter, cut to fit

F 1 straight piece, 3" to 4" in diameter, about 30" long

G 7 to 8 straight pieces, 2" to 2½" in diameter, 32" long

H 2 curved pieces, 2½" to 3" in diameter, 31" long

I 2 curved pieces, 2" to 2½" in diameter, cut to fit

J 2 straight pieces, 2" to 2½" in diameter, cut to fit

K 12 to 18 curved pieces, 1½" to 2½" in diameter, varied lengths from 21"

to 32" OR 6 to 9 pieces, 3" to 4" in diameter, varied lengths from 21" to 32"

Assorted screws and lag bolts

Assorted pieces for bracing

TOOLS

Bandsaw/jigsaw   Screwdriver

Drill and drill bits   Socket wrench

Sander

Choosing Your Wood

Ⓐ Base Supports

Find a straight solid piece in your driftwood pile, about 41" in length and 4" to 5" in diameter. The piece will need to be cut lengthwise to get the two symmetrical base supports for your chair.

Ⓑ Front Legs

You'll need a sturdy, straight piece that's 4" to 5" thick and 19" long. The single piece you're looking for here will be mirror-cut to give you two front legs.

Ⓒ Back Legs

As with the base supports and front legs, one piece cut down its length will provide the two pieces you need.

Look for a straight piece about 46" long and, again, about 4" to 5" in diameter.

Ⓓ Seat

Find seven or eight straight pieces, about 2" to 2½" in diameter and 24" in length. Ideally, the pieces you'll use will be very similar in diameter – the closer they are in size, the more comfortable you'll feel sitting in your constructed chair. Remember, longer pieces of the proper diameter can always be cut into shorter lengths.

Ⓔ Back Supports

Two nicely curved pieces will serve as your back supports. Look for two pieces about 2" to 2½" in diameter.

They will need to be at least 24" long and can be cut to fit.

F Arms

Find a reasonably straight piece about 3" to 4" in diameter and 30" long. Once mirror-cut, you'll have the arms for your chair.

G Backrest

Like the cross joiners for your seat, the pieces for your backrest should be similar in diameter to ensure better comfort while sitting in the chair. Search for seven or eight straight pieces, each about 32" long and 2" to 2½" in diameter.

H Main Hood Supports

Find two gently curved pieces for the main hood supports. Each will need to be 2½" to 3" thick and about 31" in length.

I Hood Braces

The two pieces needed for the hood braces should be curved, 2" to 2½" in diameter and at least 24" long. Try to find a piece that's on the longer end of the scale, as the amount of curve in the main hood support pieces will affect the length of the pieces needed here and you don't want to be left short when you're nearly done the project.

J Upper Hood Supports

Find two good support pieces that are slightly curved, 2" to 2½" in diameter and at least 36" long. The pieces should be strong, but need little character because they'll be mostly hidden from view.

K Roof Slats

What you are looking for in roof slats are curved pieces that vary in length from 21" to 32" (the varying lengths create the curved roofline at the front). Remember that you can always cut down pieces to create the lengths needed. As for quantity and diameter, what you're seeking depends on what type of selection you have available in your driftwood pile. Your first option is to use 12 to 18 pieces that are 1½" to 2½" in diameter. Option two is to use half as many pieces (6 to 9) that are 3" to 4" in diameter and cut them lengthwise to double your quantity.

Building Instructions

STEP 1: Putting the Frame Together

Begin with the base supports (A) and front legs (B). Start by mirror-cutting the pieces. If you've already done so, great. Just be sure the pieces haven't warped or you'll have to go searching through your driftwood pile again.

Next, predrill holes in both the base supports and front legs and use lag bolts to attach them to one another. See Fig. 1. You'll want to hold off on firmly tightening the bolts, though. Wait until after the basic frame is assembled so that you'll have a sturdy piece to work with and can level it properly. For now, the base support should be about 10" from the ground where it attaches to the front legs.

Now attach the back legs (C) to the base supports by predrilling holes and fastening with lag bolts. (Your frame isn't quite built, so don't tighten those bolts yet.) There should be 6" from where the base supports attach to the back legs. Also, the base supports should be sloping back towards the rear of the chair.

Next comes the seat assembly. Refer to Fig. 1 for guidance. You'll need to predrill holes in all pieces used thus far, as well as your seat pieces (D). For stability, secure the seat pieces at the front and back of the seat with lag bolts.

If your frame is sitting pretty, it's time to firmly tighten up all those lag bolts I told you to hold off on. To finish the seat, the remaining seat pieces can be secured into place with #10 3½" screws.

STEP 2: Assembling the Back and Arms

We'll start with the back of the chair. Grab the two pieces you'll be using for the upper and lower back supports (E). The upper support should be screwed onto the back legs about 28" to 30" up from the base.

The lower support will rest about 2" up from the seat. Take a measurement to determine what length you'll need this piece to be and then cut your selected piece to size.

To create a secure fit to the back legs, the arms (F) will have to be notched near the back. See Fig. 2. Notching may also be required to fit the arms to the front legs. Attach the arms to the frame as shown in Fig. 3. Remember that the arms should either have a slight slope back or be parallel to the ground. Predrill holes in the pieces and lag bolt the arms into place.

To finish the back of the chair, you'll need to attach your backrest pieces (G) to the two back supports. The backrest pieces will be a little closer to one another where they attach to the lower back support,

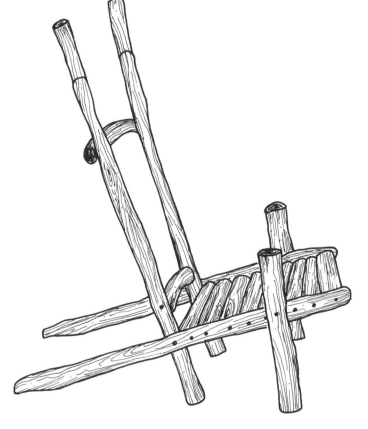

Figure 1

Figure 2

TIP See if you can gather up an assistant before starting the hood assembly. If this isn't possible, you'll likely want to lay the chair on its side to get it going.

then spread out somewhat up to where they attach to the upper back support. Use screws to secure the backrest pieces to the supports.

STEP 3: Putting Up the Hood

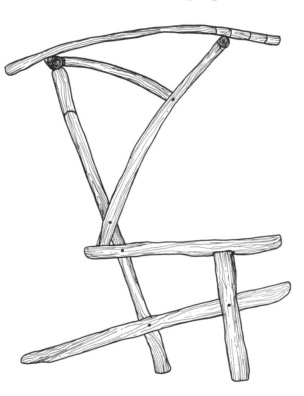

Figure 3

The trickiest part of the hood construction is starting it. You'll see why in a moment. Get the pieces you've chosen for the main hood supports (H), hood braces (I) and upper hood supports (J).

Have a look at Figs. 3 and 4 and refer to them for guidance whenever needed. Start with one side of the chair – I began with the right side – and lay out the pieces on the ground to get a sense of where each one will be going and how they'll all fit together. You may need to cut down the hood brace somewhat to get the correct fit.

To begin, attach the right main hood support to the right hood brace with screws. The main hood support is then secured on the chair frame by screwing it at its base to the arm and back legs and then screwing the hood brace to the top of the back legs. Now do the same for the left side.

Next, attach the upper hood supports (J). The rear support is screwed to the back legs and the front support is screwed to the main hood support. (If you had an assistant to this point, you can thank the person for help now and send them on their way.)

The pieces for the roof slats (K) should be lined up in the back, but curve into an arc at the front. See Fig. 4. If you're using the larger quantity of round pieces, determine exactly how many you'll need and then screw them in place. If you're mirror-cutting the pieces, however, get on the job and watch that they don't warp. Lay the pieces flat side down and screw them in place.

STEP 4: Bracing

For the sake of stability, you'll need cross bracing at the front and back of the chair, as well as bracing for the arms. Let's start at the front of the chair. As a support for the front legs, you'll need two crisscrossed pieces screwed to the front legs below the seat. Also screw the cross braces together at the point where they intersect. See Fig. 5.

Figure 4

Figure 5

Figure 6

We'll move now to the rear of the chair. Attach cross braces behind the seat, with the lower back support providing the intersection point. Ensure you screw the cross braces to each other as well as to the chair frame. See Fig. 6.

Finally, you can brace the arms for more support. Two curved pieces will act as your braces, screwed into place to the arms and the front legs on each side. See Fig. 7.

Now that the project is done, you'll have somewhere to sit while you relax and enjoy your surroundings.

Figure 7

Three-Legged Chair

Please be seated

MATERIALS

A 1 straight piece, 3" to 4" in diameter, 40" long

B 1 curved piece, about 2½" in diameter, 17" long

C 1 curved piece, 2½" to 3" in diameter, 20" long

D 1 curved piece, 3" to 4" in diameter, 18" to 20" long OR 2 matching curved pieces, about 2" in diameter, 18" to 20" long

E 2 straight pieces, 4" to 5" in diameter, about 26" long

F 1 straight piece, 2" to 3" in diameter, about 25" long

G 1 straight piece, 2" to 3" in diameter, about 20" long

H 1 curved piece, 2" to 2½" in diameter, about 20" long

I 1 straight piece, 2" to 2½" in diameter, about 20" long

J 1 curved piece, 2½" to 4" in diameter, about 20" long

K 6 to 8 straight pieces, 2½" to 3" in diameter, cut to fit

Assorted pieces for bracing

Assorted screws and lag bolts

TOOLS

Bandsaw/jigsaw

Drill and drill bits

Sander

Screwdrivers

Socket wrench

Choosing Your Wood

Ⓐ Spine

The spine is the most important piece in this project. Find a good, strong spine piece, approximately 40" long and 3" to 4" thick. For a more rustic look, and for added stability, search for a piece with a root at its base.

Ⓑ Back Support

Select a nice, gently curved piece for the back support. It should be 17" wide and approximately 2½" thick.

Ⓒ Rear Seat Rail

What you're looking for is a solid, nicely curved piece that's 20" long and 2½" to 3" in diameter.

Ⓓ Side Seat Rails

Search in your driftwood pile for two matching curved pieces, 18" to 20" long and 1½" to 2" in diameter for the side seat rails. If you can't find two similar pieces, one piece will do the trick. Just make sure it's thicker – 3" to 4" in diameter – and cut it lengthwise so you end up with two matching pieces.

❸ Front Legs

If you're fortunate, you'll find two nice front legs in your driftwood pile, maybe even with a Y-shaped top (to hold the arms). They should be 4" to 5" in diameter, preferably on the thicker end, and about 26" long.

❺ Back Verticals

Find an interesting straight piece, maybe with a root on the end (like I did), about 2" to 3" in diameter and about 25" in length. Once mirror-cut, it will form the back verticals.

❼ Front Seat Rail (not visible)

This will act as the main seat support piece. It should be 2" to 3" in diameter and about 20" in length.

❽ Front Brace (not visible)

Find a gently curved piece, about 2" to 2½" in diameter and 20" long. A curved piece is necessary because it's going to be attached at its upper arc to the front rail.

❾ Stretcher

The stretcher should be straight and solid, 2½" to 3" thick and about 20" long.

❿ Arms

Think about what shape you'd like for the arms of your chair when choosing this piece. You'll need a gently curved piece, 2½" to 4" in diameter (the wider the piece, the more resting room for your arms) and about 20" long. Ultimately, it will be mirror-cut to create two matching pieces.

ⓚ Back and Seat

Find six to eight straight pieces, 2½" to 3" in diameter. Once mirror-cut, they'll create the seat and back of your chair.

Building Instructions

Building this three-legged chair proved to be quite a challenge. Don't select it as your first or second driftwood furniture project.

STEP 1: Getting Started

Take the pieces you've chosen for your spine (A) and back support (B). Notch the back support where it will attach to the spine. See Fig. 1. Predrill holes and secure the two pieces together with a lag bolt.

Figure 1

TIP I rested the "U" on a picnic table seat until the front legs were ready for assembly.

STEP 2: Building and Attaching the "U"

To neatly fit the pieces together, you'll need to make scarf cuts at both ends of the rear seat rail (C) and one end of the side seat rails (D). See Fig. 2. (If you only have one piece for the side seat rails and haven't mirror-cut it yet, then get on with it.)

Figure 2

Use screws to attach the side seat rails to the rear seat rail. Now that the "U" is all assembled, you can prepare to attach it to the spine. Make a notch in the spine piece about 16" to 18" up from the base. Predrill holes in the rear seat rail and in the spine, and lag bolt the "U" to the spine. See Fig. 3.

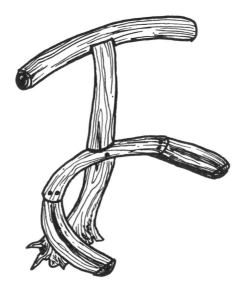

Figure 3

STEP 3: Completing the Frame

Get the pieces you're using for your front legs (E). Determine the appropriate height where they should be attached to the "U" – about 18" from the base of each leg. See Fig. 4. Predrill holes for the bolts. Make whatever cuts are necessary to the front of the "U" so it will fit securely to the front legs. Bolt together using lag bolts.

To finish the frame for the back of the seat, you'll need to mirror-cut the piece you chose for the back verticals (F). Predrill holes and use lag bolts to attach the verticals to the "U" and back support. Once again, see Fig. 4 for a visual.

On to the front of the chair. The front seat rail (G) will line up with the front of the "U." Predrill holes in the front seat rail and the front legs and attach with lag bolts. The front brace (H) will be bolted to the legs and screwed to the underside of the front seat rail. This will add greatly to the amount of weight that can be borne by the chair. Finally, the stretcher (I) is bolted to the legs at a point beneath the other two pieces. See Fig. 5.

The next step is bracing. This is particularly important, especially for the back of the "U." In the photograph on page 63 you can see how I've braced on both sides of the spine up to the middle of the sides of the "U." Predrill, then use screws to attach the bracing pieces to the frame.

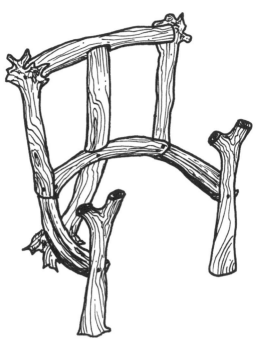

Figure 4

STEP 4: Up in Arms

Find the piece you've chosen for the arms (J). Cut it lengthwise to get two matching pieces. You'll need to finish both ends. The end that will attach to the back verticals should be notched to fit. The other end should be nicely curved. See Fig. 6. If your front legs are Y-shaped pieces, you can rest the arms in the pit of the Y; if not, just sit the arms on top of the legs. Predrill holes and lag bolt the arms to the front legs and back verticals.

STEP 5: Completing the Back and Seat

Your back and seat pieces (K) will need to be cut lengthwise if you haven't done so already. Be sure to round the fronts of the seat pieces so there aren't any awkward or pointy edges. You may also have to notch the undersides at the front of the seat pieces to make the seat nice and level. Once all is well, predrill holes and screw the pieces into the back and seat of the chair.

Take a well-deserved seat in your brand-new chair! If it feels a little rough around the edges (and it probably will) sand the back, arms and seat before setting it out for use.

TIP To create a smooth, level surface on the arms, I countersunk the lag bolts that attached the arms and front legs together.

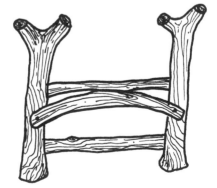

Figure 5

Figure 6

Conversation Chairs

Find a friend and relax for a chat

MATERIALS

A 4 straight pieces, 2½" to 3½" in diameter, 34" long

B 4 straight pieces, 2" to 3" in diameter, 24" to 26" long

OR 2 straight pieces, 3" to 4" in diameter, 24" to 26" long

C 2 straight pieces, 2" to 3" in diameter, 24" to 26" long

D 2 straight pieces, 2" to 3" in diameter, 22" long

E 1 straight piece, 2" to 3" in diameter, 44" long

F 2 straight pieces, 2" to 3" in diameter, 26" long

G 1 straight piece, 2" to 3" in diameter, 26" long

H 1 straight piece, 2½" to 3½" in diameter, 58" long

I 1 slightly curved piece, 3" to 5" in diameter, 22" long

J 1 straight piece, 3" to 5" in diameter, 44" long

K 6 to 8 straight pieces, 2" to 3" in diameter, 22" long

L 14 to 16 straight to slightly curved pieces, 1" to 2" in diameter, 15" to 20" long

Assorted pieces for bracing

Assorted screws and lag bolts

TOOLS

Bandsaw/jigsaw   Screwdriver

Drill and drill bits   Socket wrench

Sander

Choosing Your Wood

Ⓐ Back Legs

The back legs should be strong and sturdy pieces, 2½" to 3½" thick and about 34" long.

Ⓑ Back Supports

Each back support piece should be straight and solid. Look for four pieces that are 24" to 26" long and 2" to 3" in diameter. You can also mirror-cut two straight pieces that are 3" to 4" in diameter and 24" to 26" long to end up with the four pieces you need.

Ⓒ Rear Seat Rails

Just like the back support pieces, each rear seat rail should be 24" to 26" long and 2" to 3" in diameter.

Ⓓ Right Seat Rails

Find two straight pieces that are 2" to 3" in diameter and 22" long.

Ⓔ Common Left Seat Rail

This is the one piece that connects the "lefts" of each chair. It should be a good, solid, straight piece of wood, 2" to 3" in diameter and 44" long.

Ⓕ Right Front Legs

Search in your woodpile for two straight pieces that are 2" to 3" thick and 26" long. To add a little style to the chair, use pieces with Y-shaped ends if you have them. That way the arms will sit in the "Y."

G Common Left Front Leg

The left front leg should be 2" to 3" in diameter and 26" in length. This piece will support both chairs, so ensure it's good and solid.

H Common Front Seat Rail

Again, this piece will be shared by both chairs, so be sure it's solid and strong. It should be nice and straight, 2½" to 3½" thick and 58" long.

I Right Arms

Once mirror-cut, this piece will make the two right arms. Look for a piece that has a slight curve to it and is 3" to 5" thick and 22" long.

J Common Left Arm

This 44" long piece will be the left armrest for both chairs. It should match the width of the pieces you use for the right arms.

K Seat

You will need about six to eight pieces for the seat. Find pieces that are 2" to 3" in diameter and about 22" in length.

L Back

Look for 14 to 16 pieces, 1" to 2" in diameter and 15" to 20" long, for the back. They should be straight to slightly curved in shape.

Building Instructions

STEP 1: Creating the Chair Frame

These chairs are all-time favorites of mine. I saw a set of conversation chairs many years ago in an antique store, so I unfortunately can't say it's an original design of mine.

To get started, you'll need to construct one chair frame then the other.

As you can see in the illustration on page 69, there are four "common" pieces used for both chairs. We will get to each of those shortly.

Gather together your back legs (A), back supports (B) and rear seat rails (C). As you're building one chair frame at a time, set the extra pieces aside until you start working on chair number two.

To keep things simple, all joints in the frame should be secured with lag bolts. The seat should be about 16" to 18" off the ground, so attach the rear seat rail accordingly. If you are using a round piece rather than a mirror-cut piece for the back support, be sure to sand it smooth for comfort.

Attach the right seat rail (D) to what you have assembled so far. Then it's time to attach the common left seat rail (E). This will stretch a long distance past the frame of the chair you are constructing and will ultimately be part of the second chair.

Next, secure the right front leg (F) and common left front leg (G) in place with lag bolts. Then attach the common front seat rail (H) to complete the frame of the first chair. See Fig. 1. You can now move on to finish the frame of the second chair by repeating the above steps. Do your best to match the look of the first chair, especially the back supports.

After you have finished the full chair frame, you can tackle the bracing. The photograph on page 68 shows you how to simply and effectively brace these chairs. Try to pick out some good, solid pieces for the braces. Once you've added some bracing, rock the frame a bit to see how it's holding up. Don't hesitate to add more bracing if you need to. Remember, these chairs could be holding two 250-pound people. Be sure the whole structure is good and solid.

STEP 2: Completing the Chair

The arms can be introduced now. The two right arms (I) are mirror-cut from the same piece of wood and will look best if they curve slightly outward (as in the photograph on page 68). The cut, or flat side should face up. Be sure to sand the cut side smooth. Also, when joining, countersink the lag bolt for better comfort.

Next, you will attach the common left arm (J). First mirror-cut the piece and sand it smooth. Although you will only need one of the cut pieces, it's necessary to do the cut so the piece matches the right arms and provides better comfort while you're resting. Once again, countersink the lag bolt.

For the seat (K), mirror-cut all the pieces and sand them smooth. Be sure to screw them in place with the flat sides up.

Finally, complete the backs of the chairs. The back pieces (L) may need to be cut to fit. Screw each back piece to both the rear seat rail and back support of each chair. I found that you can make a more comfortable back if you attach the back pieces behind the back supports.

Now find a person you like to sit and talk with and get using these chairs.

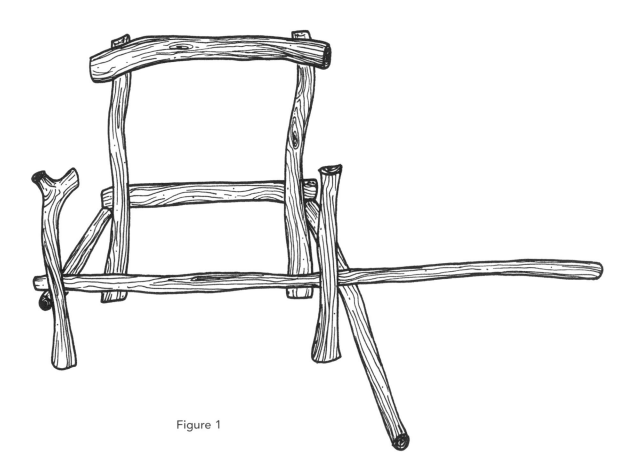

Figure 1

Chaise Longue

Lie back and enjoy

MATERIALS

A 2 straight pieces, 2½" to 3" in diameter, 6½' long

B 1 straight piece, 2½" to 3" in diameter, 6½' long

OR 2 straight pieces, 2½" to 3" in diameter, 3¼' long

C 2 straight pieces, 2½" to 3" in diameter, 5½' long

D 2 straight or curved pieces, 2½" to 3" in diameter, 20" to 24" long

E 2 straight pieces, 1½" to 2" in diameter, about 3½' long

F 24 to 30 straight pieces, 1" in diameter, about 3' long

G 3 straight pieces, 2" in diameter, about 3' long

H 1 straight or Y-shaped piece, 2" to 3" in diameter, about 3' long

I 2 curved pieces, 2" in diameter, 4' to 5' long

J 2 straight pieces, 2½" to 3" in diameter, 5½' long

K 2 straight pieces, 1½" to 2½" in diameter, 24" to 28" long

L 1 curved piece, 2" in diameter, about 3' long

M 4 curved pieces, 1½" to 2" in diameter, about 12" to 18" long

N 2 straight pieces, 1½" to 2" in diameter, about 3' long

Assorted pieces for bracing

Assorted "character" pieces for the canopy

Assorted screws and lag bolts

Steel rod (optional)

2 wheels

TOOLS

Bandsaw/jigsaw

Drill and drill bits   Screwdriver

Sander   Socket wrench

Choosing Your Wood

Ⓐ Base Supports

This project requires strong and solid base supports. Find two hard wood lengths that are good and thick, about 2½" to 3" in diameter, and 6½' long.

Ⓑ Cross Joiners

You have two options for the cross joiners. If you happen to find a third matching piece when you're looking for the base supports – that is, one that's straight, about 2½" to 3" in diameter and 6½' long – you can cut it in half to create the cross joiners. Otherwise, find two shorter pieces of the same diameter.

Ⓒ Main Canopy Supports

Again, you're looking for good, hard wood for the canopy supports. Find two straight pieces, 5½' in length and 2½" to 3" thick.

Ⓓ Legs

You'll only need to find two pieces for the legs of the chaise longue since the rear legs are also the canopy supports. These 2½" to 3" thick, 20" to 24" long pieces can be straight or curved, but as you can see in the photograph on the oppostie page, you may want to use a piece that has a bend in it as it will contribute to the look of the chaise and make for a more interesting base for the footrest.

> **Note:** The chaise longue was made for someone about 5'6" tall. If you are making it for anyone taller you will need to adjust some of the measurements.

E Cross Supports

For your cross supports, find two straight pieces, 1½" to 2" in diameter and about 3½' long – they may need to be trimmed to fit.

F Slats

Gather about 24 to 30 straight pieces that are 1" in diameter and about 3' long for the slats. The exact number you'll need depends on how closely together you choose to place them on the frame of the chaise longue.

G Headrest Frame (not visible)

You will need three straight pieces for the frame of the headrest, each piece about 2" in diameter and 3' in length. Like the cross supports (E), they may need to be trimmed to fit.

H Headrest Support (not visible)

Although a Y-shaped piece is handy for the headrest support, if you really can't spare one or just don't have one, a straight piece will do. Whether straight or Y-shaped, the piece should be 2" to 3" thick and about 3' in length.

I Main Canopy Frame

Find two nicely curved pieces for the main canopy frame, about 2" in diameter and 4' to 5' long.

J Secondary Canopy Supports

For the secondary canopy supports, you'll want pieces that are like the main canopy supports (C) – look for straight pieces, 2½" to 3" in diameter and 5½' long.

K Canopy Cross Joiners

You will need two strong, straight pieces, 24" to 28" in length and from 1½" to 2½" thick.

L Rear Cross Joiner

For the rear cross joiner find a curved piece about 2" in diameter and 3' long. This may be a little long for your needs, but can be cut to fit.

M Canopy Braces

You'll use four curved pieces, 1½" to 2" thick and about 12" to 18" long, for the canopy braces.

N Footrest

Find two straight pieces that are 1½" to 2" in diameter and roughly 3' long.

Building Instructions

STEP **1**: Constructing the Frame

To start assembling the basic frame you'll need your base supports (A) and cross joiners (B). A half-lap joint will give you the strongest connection. See Fig. 1.

Predrill holes and securely lag bolt the pieces together using at least 4" or 5" bolts at the corners. You should also round and sand the corners for looks and safety.

Next, attach the main canopy supports (C) and legs (D). Your aim is to have the frame rest about 8" to 10" off the ground. You'll have to notch all four pieces so they will fit snugly against the assembled frame. Once measured and notched, lag bolt them in place.

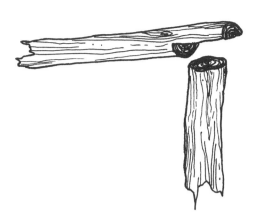

Figure 1

Finally, screw the cross supports (E) onto the canopy supports.

Now look at the bracing of the legs. This is a very important stage – make sure they're solid as a rock. I always imagine that someone weighing around 250 pounds will plunk

themselves onto the chaise. Don't let them down. Refer to Figs. 2 and 3 to see how I've done my bracing.

STEP 2: Covering the Frame

The slats (F) will cover the frame of the chaise longue. As written in the Choosing Your Wood section, the number that you need depends on how closely together you choose to place them. If you're planning on putting a cushion on it as I did (see page 72), you can space the slats a few inches apart. However, if you are going to be lying directly on the slats, you should space them less than an inch apart – or even butt them up one against the other – to give a better comfort level on the chaise.

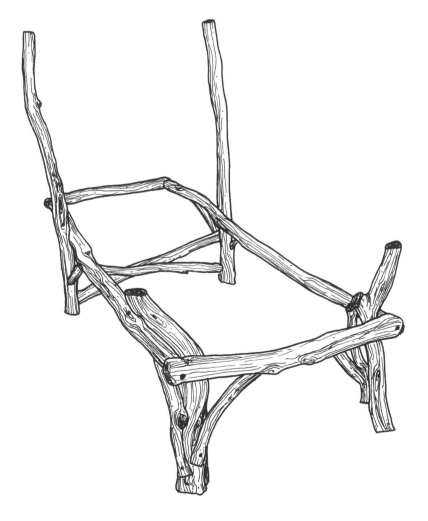

Figure 2

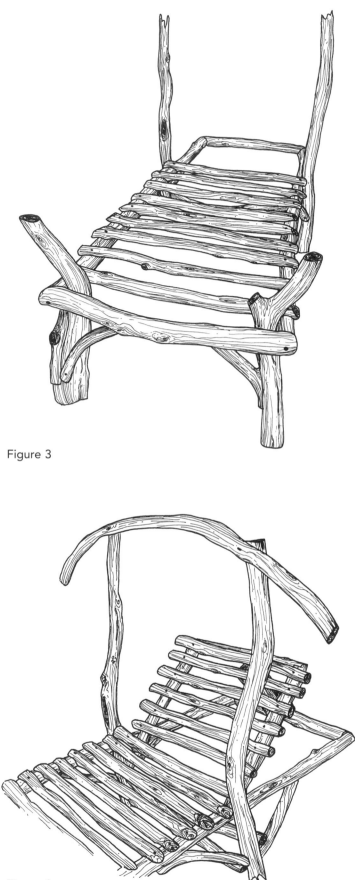

Figure 3

Figure 4

Screw a bunch of the slats (F) in place up to the tilting headrest. See Fig. 3. You'll attach the remaining slats after the headrest is built. Once again, these pieces will need to be notched to fit securely against the frame. Be sure to round off the ends for comfort.

STEP 3: Assembling the Headrest

The tilting headrest is made up of a frame that fits inside the main chaise frame. See Fig. 4. Gather your headrest frame pieces (G) and cut them to fit in the main frame. Bolt the pieces together. You can attach the assembled headrest frame to the main frame by hinging with a steel rod or, as I did, with lag bolts at the junction where it adjoins the already installed cross supports.

To allow the headrest to stay in a tilted position, you'll need to attach a support. Get your headrest support piece (H) and a few offcuts and assemble (as shown in Fig. 6). If you have a Y-shaped piece, the single end will attach to the main frame and the Y-shaped end will support the headrest.

Finish the headrest by attaching the remaining slats. These slats will be screwed to the headrest frame, not the main frame, of course.

STEP 4: Up Goes the Canopy

To start the real work on the canopy, attach one of the main canopy frame pieces (I) to the canopy supports using lag bolts. See Fig. 5. Then attach the secondary canopy supports (J) using bolts, and cap off with the second main canopy frame piece. To "square" off the canopy, attach the canopy cross joiners (K). To provide a little support, you'll need to attach the rear cross joiner (L); and for additional support, attach the canopy braces (M) to the main canopy frame and canopy supports (the canopy braces may need to be cut to fit). Refer back to the illustration on page 73 for guidance.

To finish, fill the canopy frame will all sorts of "character" pieces – use root pieces and others with interesting shapes until you reach the desired effect. Stand back and take a gander every once in a while until you think it looks well balanced and complete. Or, for a different look – and one that will perhaps provide more shade – you could attach straight lengths close together, as is done with the Hooded Chair (see Fig. 4 on page 61).

STEP 5: Finishing Touches

To complete the chaise longue, bolt or screw the footrest pieces (N) to the legs. Finally, because this piece of furniture is awfully heavy to move around, it makes good sense to add wheels to the rear legs so you can roll the chaise from place to place. See Fig. 6.

If you'd like, you can also attach a basket on the side, as I did, that can hold books or newspapers. And a nice cushioned seat will make you want to lounge with a cool drink after a project well done.

Figure 5

Figure 6

Small Table

A little table with dozens of uses

MATERIALS

A 2 boards, 1" to 1½" thick, 5" to 6" wide, 24" long

B 2 boards, at least 1" thick, 3" to 4" wide, 10" long

C 4 slightly curved pieces, 2" to 2½" in diameter, 12" to 14" long

D 1 straight piece, 2" to 2½" in diameter, 44" long

E 2 slightly curved pieces, about 2" in diameter, 24" to 26" long, and 2 straight pieces, 2" in diameter, 12" to 14" long

Assorted small pieces for bracing

Assorted screws and lag bolts

TOOLS

Bandsaw/jigsaw

Drill and drill bits

Sander/sanding block

Screwdriver

Socket wrench

Choosing Your Wood

Ⓐ Table Top

You may have difficulty finding these two boards as driftwood. Now and again you'll come across a few. Who knows where they came from – maybe some docks broke up in a storm. Nevertheless, in driftwood form they end up nicely weathered and very usable.

Failing to find such boards sent me elsewhere to look for a suitable supply. As luck would have it, I discovered a stack of crates that had been sitting for decades outside a local lumber company. They were exceptionally hard and had a lovely gray patina similar to my driftwood.

Ⓑ Table Top Joiners (not visible)

These can be made out of pieces similar to the table top (A), but they don't need to be as big. If you're really stuck, keep in mind that the joiners will be underneath the table top and never seen, so if you need to use some planks you have lying around, so be it. Just ensure they're at least 1" thick and about 10" long. (See Fig. 1.)

Ⓒ Legs

See if you can find four interesting pieces that have a slight curve. Knobby remnants or a root at one end will add greatly to the rustic charm of the final table.

Ⓓ Rails

If you can find a nice straight piece that's 44" long, then when you mirror-cut the piece length-wise, you will have enough wood to finish all four rails of the table top.

Raised Bird Feeder

Your table can double as a bird feeder by adding on this small piece.

You'll need:

a 2 straight pieces, 2" in diameter, 4" to 6" long

b 1 board, 1" thick, 3" to 4" wide, about 6" to 8" long

c 1 straight piece, 1" in diameter, 10" to 14" long

Assorted screws and lag bolts

Predrill holes into both ends of the two thick leg pieces (a) and into the table top, so the feeder will be ultimately be placed as in the photo on page 78. Screw or bolt the feeder legs to the table top.

Next, predrill holes in the platform board (b) and attach to the legs with screws or lag bolts. Finally, cut the thin straight piece (c) into two lengths that correspond with the length of the edges of the platform. Mirror-cut the pieces and screw all four to the platform to create a ledge.

Just add birdseed and wait for the flock to arrive.

ⓔ Stretchers

The two lengths that will join the legs of the long sides of the table should be nicely curved, about 24" long and 2" thick, while the two pieces for the short sides should be straight, 2" thick and 12" to 14" long.

Building Instructions

STEP 1: Topping it Up

Start by getting your two table top boards (A). For each board, have a look at the flat sides and determine which should be the top. Then lay the two boards side by side onto your working surface with the top sides down. This will give you a final table top size of about 12" by 24".

You'll notice in the photograph of the table on page 78 that I rounded the corners of the table top. This is not essential – you can leave them square. I did it because I preferred the look. If you do decide to round them, just mark a curve on each corner using a pencil and a can or cup as a guide. Cut out the curve with your jigsaw or bandsaw and sand the edges smooth.

Lay the pieces for your table top joiners (B) on the underside of the table top boards. See Fig. 1. Screw the joiners down with at least four to six screws each. Be sure you don't screw them right through the surface of the table.

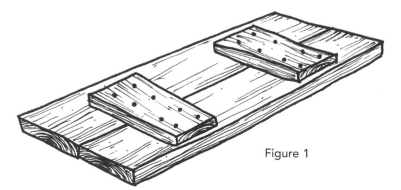

Figure 1

STEP 2: Having Four Legs to Stand on

Now you can attach the legs (C). Ensure each leg is equidistant from the corners. I arranged for the curve of the legs to be directed outwards (see the photo on page 78), but you might want to have the curve turn inwards for a very different look. It's your choice.

Predrill holes in the table top and legs and secure a leg to each corner with lag bolts. Whether you want to countersink the lag bolts or not is up to you. I didn't.

STEP 3: Edging and Strengthening

Time to add the rails (D). If you haven't done so already, it's time to mirror-cut the pieces.

To make it easier, you will probably want to cut the 44" piece into two shorter pieces. Get measurements for each side of the table – they will be approximately 12" and 24" – and cut the piece accordingly. Then mirror-cut each of the two pieces and you'll have your four rails. Screw on each rail using about six screws for each of the longer sides and about four screws for the shorter sides.

Now you're ready to give the table some support with the stretchers (E). Screw the pieces into place. Next, turn the whole table over, right side up. If the table isn't as solid as you like, add a brace or two. You'll want any bracing to be in an unconspicuous place, like from the bottom of the table center to each leg where the stretchers meet.

This finished table can be left as is or you can add the raised bird feeder to give it an extra use in your garden.

Signpost

Garden Stand

Trellis

Four-Legged Chair

Hooded Chair

Three-Legged Chair

Conversation Chairs

Chaise Longue

Small Table

Garden Bench

Wheelbarrow

Tricycle

Sleigh

Hanging Flowerbox

Arbor

Boat

Wine Rack Table

A place to store your vino, if you please

MATERIALS

A 6 straight pieces, 1 ½" in diameter, 17" long

B 4 straight pieces (can be slightly curved at the bottom), 2" to 3" in diameter, 30" long

C 2 straight pieces, 2" in diameter, 24" long

D 2 straight pieces, 2" in diameter, 13" long

E 6 straight pieces, 1 ½" to 2" in diameter, 12" long

F 6 straight pieces, 1 ½" in diameter, 18" long

G 20 to 24 pieces, 1" in diameter, 14" long

Assorted curved pieces for bracing

Assorted screws

TOOLS

Bandsaw/jigsaw

Drill and drill bits

Sander

Sanding block

Screwdriver

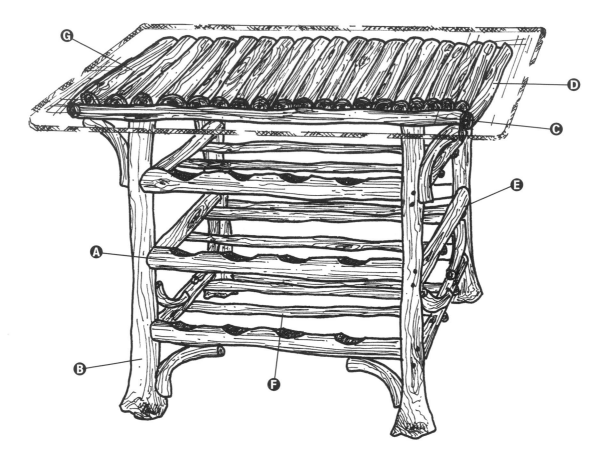

Choosing Your Wood

Ⓐ Front and Rear Stretchers

You'll need a total of six straight pieces, 1½" in diameter and 17" long. Three of these will be notched to carry the neck of the bottles and three will sit at the back, serving as a stop to keep the bottles from sliding out of the back of the table.

Ⓑ Legs

Choose these carefully because they will carry a lot of weight and must hold everything together securely – they should be no less than 2" in diameter. For the front legs, it will add to the looks if the bottoms curve out slightly – and match. If you are lucky enough to find four with similar shaping, so much the better. A length of 30" should give you a nice table height

Ⓒ Front and Rear Rails

The straighter the better for these – look for hard wood with a 2" diameter and that's 24" long.

Ⓓ Side Rails

Again, look for 2" pieces that are as straight as possible, though these will be shorter – only 13" in length.

Ⓔ Side Stretchers

To join the front frame to the back frame, you'll need six straight pieces, 12" long and 1½" to 2" thick.

❻ Bottle Rack

Your bottles will rest on these six straight pieces. The length of these will best be determined when your frame is assembled, but you're looking to find approximately 18"-long pieces that are about 1½" in diameter.

❼ Table Top

The table will be completed with 20 to 24 pieces screwed in on top. Each will need to be as close as to 1" in diameter as possible, and cut to 14" long.

Building Instructions

STEP 1: Constructing the Frames

Take three of your six stretchers (A) and notch them using your bandsaw according to the measurements in Fig. 1. These will be the front stretchers (the remaining three will be the rear stretchers). As they will only be supporting the neck of a bottle, the notches will only need to be about 1" long and about ½" deep.

Now notch the ends of all six front and rear stretchers so they'll fit snugly against the legs (B). See Fig. 2. You'll use #10 – 3½" screws to attach the stretchers to the legs. The bottom stretcher will be 12" from the base of the legs, and each other stretcher will be spaced 4½" apart. See Figs. 3 and 4.

Now add the front and rear rails (C) to these frames. They will overhang, as can be seen in Figs. 3 and 4. Again, use #10 – 3½" screws. You may want to create a couple of notches in the rails at the juncture where they sit on top of the legs so they fit more securely.

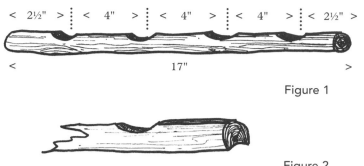

<< 2½" >> < 4" > < 4" > < 4" > < 2½" >

< 17" >

Figure 1

Figure 2

STEP 2: Joining the Frames Together

Find your two side rails (D) and notch them on all four ends to fit snugly against the front and rear rails to form the frame of the table top. Use #8 – 3½" screws.

You'll need to notch the ends of all six side stretchers (E) to give them a snug fit with the legs. The side stretchers will be placed ½" lower than the front and rear stretchers. Use #10 – 3½" screws to secure the side stretchers in place. This will give the assembly some stability.

Figure 3

Figure 4

STEP 3: Racking and Bracing

The core of the wine rack can now be completed. Confirm the length needed for the bottle rack pieces (F) and cut the six pieces to fit. Screw the rack pieces to the undersides of the side stretchers according to the measurements in Fig. 5.

Now that the base of the table is assembled, check it for stability. Add bracing and use as much as you feel is needed. You will want to make it as solid as you possibly can – this table will be holding glass bottles after all.

STEP 4: Completing the Top

There are a number of table top options but this one is the cheapest. Gather together the pieces you've chosen for your table top (G). Confirm your measurements and ensure that each piece is cut to fit. To create a more even table surface, you might want to notch the undersides of each piece. Then simply screw each piece in place.

Instead of driftwood, acrylic or plexiglass can be used. Order it from your local hardware store – they will cut and polish the edges for a small extra fee. An advantage of acrylic is that it can be drilled and secured in place. However, it is prone to getting scratched.

Glass can be very attractive, too. If you will be using the table inside, you can have the edges beveled and polished. Use grips to anchor the top in place. If you intend to use it outside, however, I'd suggest that the glass be tempered and edged in a metal frame to protect it.

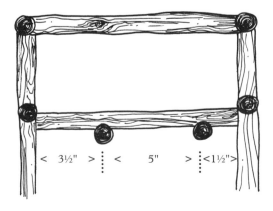

Figure 5

Patio Table

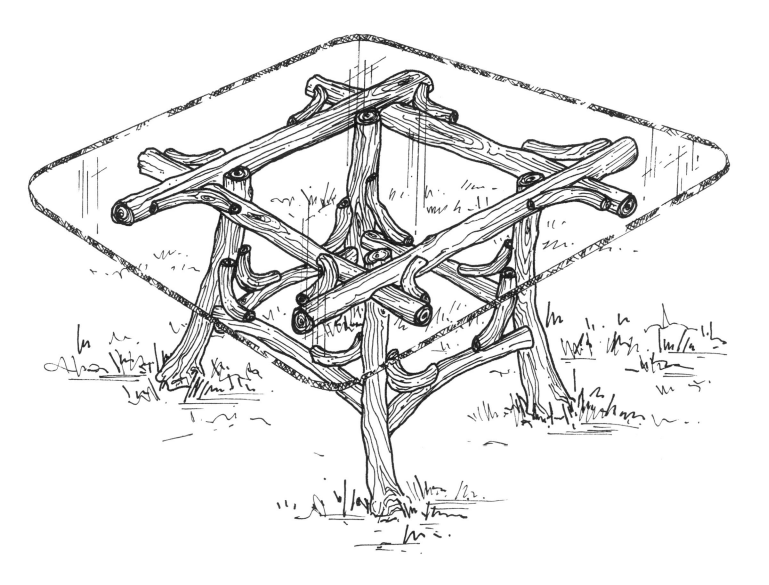

A handsome addition to any patio

MATERIALS		TOOLS
A 4 straight pieces, 2½" in diameter, 36" long	Assorted pieces for bracing	Bandsaw/jigsaw
	Assorted screws and lag bolts	Drill and drill bits
B 4 gently curved pieces, 2½" to 3" in diameter, 32" to 33" long	Glass, plexiglass or acrylic tabletop	Sander
		Screwdriver
C 4 straight or curved pieces, 2" in diameter, 30" to 36" long		Socket wrench
		Vice grips or clamps

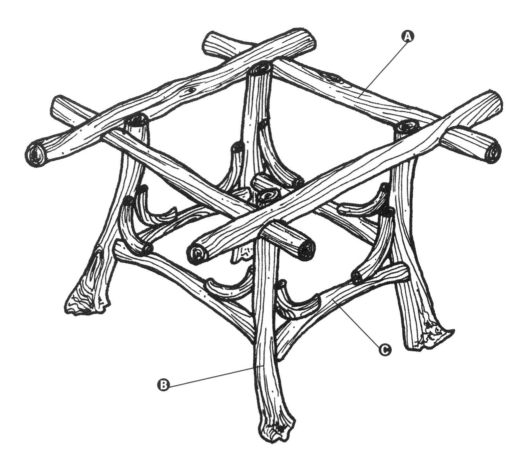

Choosing Your Wood

Ⓐ Rails

These four pieces will support the glass or acrylic table top. Make sure you select four strong, straight pieces approximately 36" long and 2½" thick.

Ⓑ Legs

The four 32" to 33" legs will give more appeal to the overall looks of the table if they are similar in shape and color. If you are fortunate enough to have four with the remnants of worn roots at one end, it will add a great deal to the rustic look of this project. Each leg should be no less that 2½" thick.

Ⓒ Stretchers

The four pieces that join the legs together at the bottom can be curved or straight, depending on what you have in your woodpile. They should be about 2" thick and 30" to 36" in length.

Building Instructions

STEP 1: Assembling the Frame

Get the pieces you have chosen for your rails (A). You will need to notch two of these, about 7" from each end, so they will fit snugly on top of the other two pieces. See. Fig. 1.

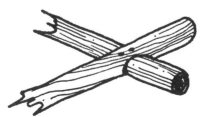

Figure 1

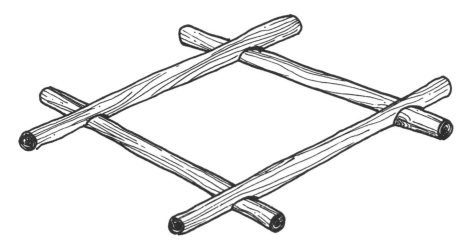

Figure 2

To assemble, turn all the pieces over and lag bolt from underneath on an angle that will enable a longer bolt to be used. Doing it this way will eliminate bolt heads from sticking up where the acrylic or glass table top will ultimately lay. See Fig. 2.

Brace all the outside joints with small, curved pieces of wood. Be sure to keep the frame as square as possible. See Fig. 3.

Put the frame you have constructed face down on your workbench. Position one of the legs (B) on one of the inside corners of the table frame. (Note: If the legs are very straight, you may want to place them on the outside corners of the frame, as in Fig. 4.) Connect the leg to each side of the frame using lag bolts.

Either have someone hold the leg in position, or else prop it up and

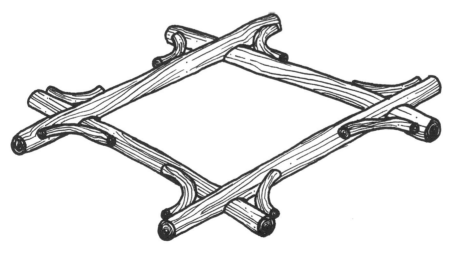

Figure 3

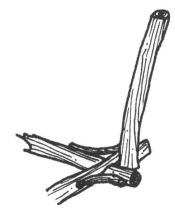

Figure 4

STEP 2: Attaching the Legs and Stretchers

Although this may seem like a relatively easy project compared to some of the other ones in this book, don't rush it. You should particularly take your time on this very important step.

clamp it then go on to the second leg. Once it's secured, you can drill and bolt one of the stretchers (C) and use it to connect the two legs together. See Fig. 5.

Next you will attach the third leg and second stretcher. This stretcher

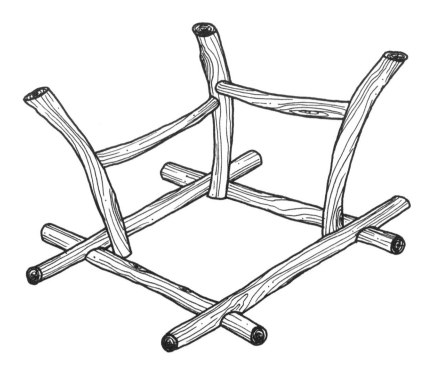

Figure 5

should be attached closer to the frame of the table so the stretcher height is staggered (refer again to Fig. 5).

Lastly, install the fourth leg, and the third and fourth stretchers. The third stretcher should be attached at the same leg height as the first; and the fourth at the same leg height as the second.

STEP 3: Leveling the Table

Now turn the framework right side up and place it on a level surface. If the table rocks a bit, you may need to trim some of the legs to get the table even. This is also the time to ensure all legs uniformly angle out. Adjust if necessary by repositioning the lag bolts to the table top frame.

Complete the bracing of the table, as seen in the illustration on page 102. When this is complete, do a last check to see if the table is rock steady – especially if it is going to have a glass table top.

STEP 4: Adding the Table Top

This table was designed for use with a glass, plexiglass or acrylic table top. The choice is up to you. If you decide on acrylic, it can be attached by drilling and screwing it to the tops of the table legs. Remember that acrylic expands, so ensure that you drill large enough holes to allow for this expansion. You can use ¼"-thick or ½"-thick acrylic.

If you use glass or plexiglass, it should be a minimum of ¼" thick. Little rubber cushions can be glued to the tops of the legs to support the glass. As well, if it's going to be an outdoor table, you should use tempered glass with a metal frame. For inside use, polished or beveled glass will suffice.

The shape of the table top is up to you. Fortunately, the square-shaped table base lends to a variety of shapes for the top, including rectangular, square, oval or round.

Garden Bench

The perfect place to sit and relax in your garden

MATERIALS

A 2 slightly curved pieces, 2" to 3" in diameter, about 36" long

B 1 curved piece, 2½" to 3" in diameter, about 66" long

C 1 straight piece, 2" to 3" in diameter, about 66" long

D 1 J-shaped piece, 2" to 3" in diameter, about 40" long

E 2 straight pieces, 2" to 3" in diameter, about 22" long

F 2 slightly curved pieces (Y-shaped optional), 2" to 3" in diameter, 24" to 26" long

G 1 straight piece, 2" to 3" in diameter, about 66" long

H 2 straight pieces, 2½" to 3" in diameter, about 22" long

OR 1 straight piece, 5" to 6" in diameter, about 22" long

I 16 to 18 curved pieces, 1½" to 2" in diameter, varying lengths (depending on the design you choose)

J 24 to 30 straight pieces, 1½" to 2" in diameter, 24" long

K 1 straight piece, 3" in diameter, about 17" long (optional)

Assorted screws and lag bolts

Assorted small pieces for bracing

TOOLS

Bandsaw/jigsaw

Drill and drill bits

Level

Sanding block/sander

Screwdriver

Socket wrench

Vice grips or clamps

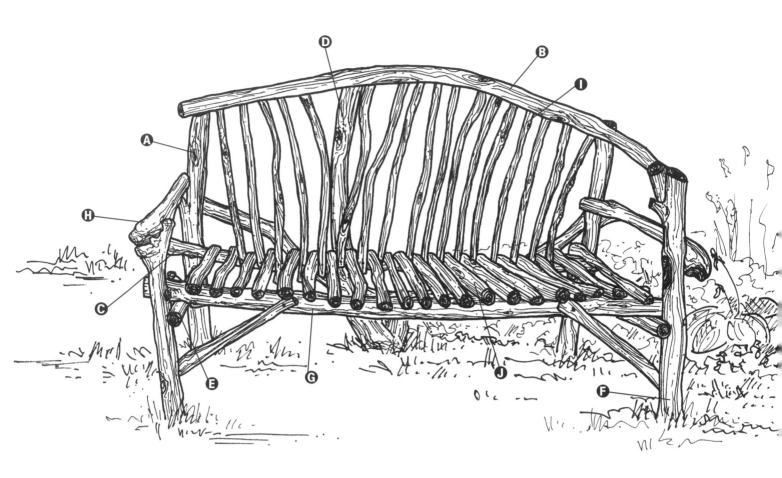

Choosing Your Wood

Ⓐ Back Legs

The legs are best if they have a bit of a curve in them that closely matches each other. If you are lucky, so may have one or two that have a forked top that can be used to rest the back top into the forks. The "Y" shape will give you the best support and is easier to attach. The crotch of the "Y" will have to be curved at the junction with your jigsaw to accommodate the back top. The length of the legs will be determined by the height that you want the back to be. I have found that 36" works well.

Ⓑ Back Support

Check your pile of longer pieces of driftwood for a nice piece that is hard and smooth, and has an interesting curve. It should be at least 66" long and 2½" to 3½" in diameter. It can be thicker at one end, which will often be the case.

Ⓒ Rear Seat Rail

It should be about 66" long, fairly straight and 2" to 3" thick.

Ⓓ Back Brace

The challenge will be to find a piece of driftwood that has the right curve. It should curve from the middle of the back support (B) to the rear seat rail (C) and on down to the ground beyond the back legs (A).

ⓔ Side Seat Rails

They should be similar to the front and rear seat rails, fairly straight and only about 22" long. These can be shortened if necessary.

ⓕ Front Legs

The two front legs should be selected carefully. Ideally, they should be somewhat straight at the bottom (from the seat down) and curve slightly outward at the top. If you are lucky, you will find one or two with a Y-shaped top so you will have a good, firm base to attach the arms.

ⓖ Front Seat Rail

Like the rear seat rail, it should be fairly straight, about 66" in length and 2" to 3" in diameter.

ⓗ Arms

These are what people will lean on, lift the bench by and feel with their hands while sitting. Depending on your choice of pieces, they can give a wonderful finish to your bench. Therefore, they should be strong, smooth, properly secured and have an interesting shape. If you can't find two pieces that will do the trick, you can always cut one piece of good driftwood in half lengthwise to form the two matching arms (placing the flat side on top).

ⓘ Back

The back design should be confirmed at this point. If you decide to use straight, vertical pieces, it will have to be braced; if you choose a fan or sunray design, then these pieces will give you all the bracing you need.

ⓙ Seat

I have tried using long pieces installed lengthwise as well as short pieces front to back. I prefer placing them front to back, as it's generally easier to find these lengths. If you want to save on material and cut back on the bench's weight, cut these short pieces lengthwise and lay the flat side down. If some pieces are thicker than others, you can also trim them lengthwise to make them roughly the same size as the others.

ⓚ Middle Leg (optional – not visible)

For additional safety and strength, I sometimes add a middle leg on the front seat support. To determine if this is necessary, you can place a small plank across the middle of the seat and gently sit on it. If it sags, then take the extra effort to put on a middle leg. It will also need to be properly braced on three sides.

Note: This project was profiled on pages 28–32.

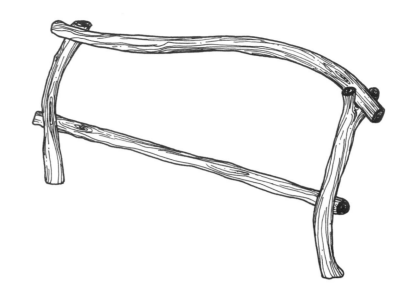

Figure 1

Building Instructions

STEP 1: Assembling the Back Frame

First, lay your two back legs (A) on the ground about 60" apart and position the back support (B) on the legs. Allow about 2" or 3" of the back support to extend beyond the legs on each side. Lag bolt these together either to the front or to the top of the legs. If you are going to attach them to the front, then notch to fit for extra strength. If the back support is curved, allow it to slope upwards and backwards; this will provide more comfort, as well as a nicer appearance. See Fig. 1. If you are fortunate enough to find one or two back legs with Y-shaped tops, then you can bolt the back support to them. Notch a curve in the bottom of the "Y" with a jigsaw for a better, snugger fit.

Lay the rear seat rail (C) in position behind the back legs – the top of which will be 17" from the ground. Mark the seat rails and notch them. Now lag bolt them to the backs of the legs. Ensure that the seat rail extends 3" past each leg, similar to the back support.

Next you can attach the back brace (D), making sure that the bottom of the brace protrudes further back than the two back legs. Notch, drill and lag bolt to the back support and rear seat rail.

STEP 2: The Frame Comes Together

Find the two pieces you've selected for your side seat rails (E) – designate one as your "right" and the other as your "left." Position the right seat rail against the back right leg directly under the rear seat rail. Notch, drill and lag bolt to the back right leg. Repeat for the left seat rail.

Figure 2

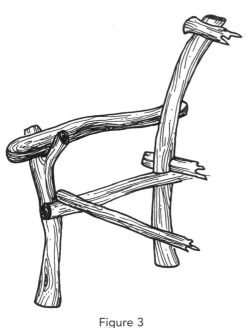

Figure 3

Decide which of your front legs (F) will be the "right" and "left." Place the right front leg against the right seat rail so that the seat rail is parallel to the ground and meets the right front leg at a 90-degree angle. Notch, drill and bolt. Repeat for the left front leg.

Position the front seat rail (G) on top of the side seat rails behind the front legs, as shown in Fig. 2. Clamp the rail to the legs, then step back and check that the seat is level and parallel to the ground – use a level if you wish. Adjust as necessary. When everything is level, notch, drill and lag bolt the front seat rail to the front legs.

Time to attach the arms (H). Position the right arm against the back leg about 24" from the ground. If the tops of the front legs are Y-shaped, then by all means set the arms in these. See Fig. 3. Notch, drill and either lag bolt or screw (#10 screws) to the leg. The front of the arm should project over the top of the front leg and be secured with two #10 screws or a lag bolt (countersunk for comfort). Repeat for the left arm.

You have now completed the frame. It should look like the diagram in Fig. 4.

TIP Try to avoid notching the legs. Instead, notch the pieces that will be attached to the legs.

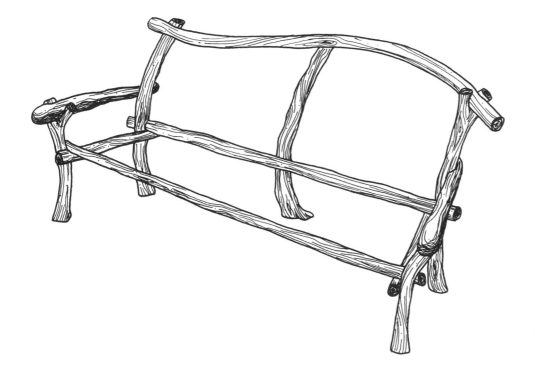

Figure 4

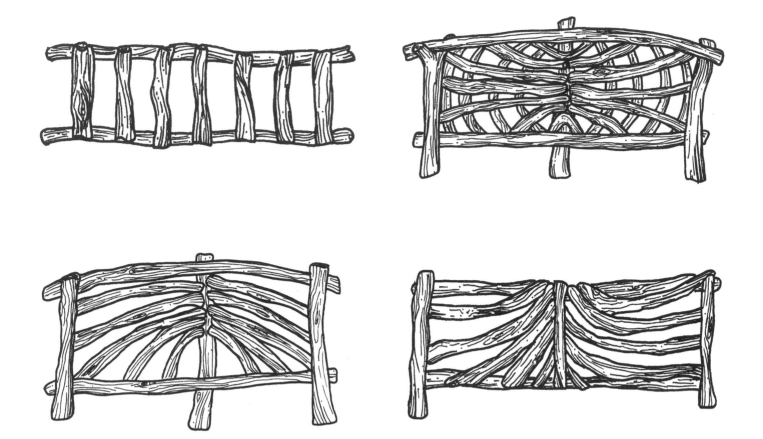

Figure 5

STEP 3: Completing the Bench

If you haven't decided on what kind of back you want, there's no time like the present! Look at Fig. 5 for some ideas. Attach the back pieces (I) to the back support and rear seat rail according to your design. Remember, if you are using straight, vertical pieces, the back will have to be braced, but if you choose a fan or sunray design, then you won't require any further bracing. Next, attach the seat pieces (J) to the front and rear seat rails according to your design preference.

Finally, sit on the bench and try rocking it from side to side and front to back. Is it solid? If not, you should attach a middle leg (K) to the middle of the front seat rail. Use two small curved pieces to brace the middle leg. Continue bracing corners where necessary to add strength and decoration.

Wheelbarrow

A lovely decoration in any yard

MATERIALS

A 2 mostly straight pieces, 2½" to 3" in diameter, about 60" long

B 2 straight pieces, 2½" to 3" in diameter, one 18" long and the other 30" long OR 1 straight piece, 2½" to 3" in diameter, 48" long

C 4 straight or curved pieces, 2" in diameter, 6" to 8" long

D 4 straight or curved pieces, 2" in diameter, cut to fit

E 25 to 30 straight pieces, 1" to 1½" in diameter, 6" to 8" long

F 3 or 4 straight pieces, 2" in diameter, cut to fit
  OR 2 to 3 flat pieces, cut to fit

G 2 straight pieces, 2" to 3" in diameter, 8" to 12" long

Iron wheel, 14" in diameter

Axle (pre-existing or a long bolt secured with a nut)

Assorted curved pieces for bracing

Assorted screws and lag bolts

TOOLS

Bandsaw/jigsaw

Drill and drill bits

Rasp (optional)

Sander

Screwdriver

Socket wrench

Choosing Your Wood

Ⓐ Handles

For the handles, select two matching pieces from your woodpile, about 60" long. Whereas they don't have to be perfectly straight, they should be similar, and must be strong pieces about 2½" to 3" in diameter. If you can find pieces that taper a little, too, all the better.

Ⓑ Cross Braces (not visible)

The two cross braces should be straight, and about 2½" to 3" in diameter. Their size will depend on the width of the wheel and length of the axle – and also how straight or curved your handles are – but to be safe, ensure one piece is at least 18" long and the other is at least 30" long. You can also use one long piece, about 48" long and cut to the lengths you need. See Fig. 1.

Ⓒ Basket Uprights

Find four straight or curved pieces that are about 2" in diameter and 6" to 8" in length.

Ⓓ Rails

These four pieces will need to be about 2" in diameter. Their lengths will ultimately correspond to the lengths of the cross braces, as well as the distance between them, so you can't be sure of the exact measure until you get to the middle stages of this project. Ideally, just have a couple of long lengths of 2"-thick wood that you can cut to fit, or an assortment of pieces that are anywhere from about 20" to 30" long.

❺ Basket Sides

You will require 25 to 30 straight pieces, 1" to 1½" thick and 6" to 8" long, to fill in the sides of the basket.

❻ Floor

The key rule to remember for your floor pieces is that they need to be strong. If you end up using your wheelbarrow to hold flowerpots, they will need to support their weight – and those pots can get quite heavy when the soil gets waterlogged after a heavy rainfall. You can use three to four straight pieces of driftwood that are about 2" in diameter or else a couple of thick, flat pieces of weathered wood. In either case, their lengths will need to be cut to fit.

❼ Legs

The legs will hold a good deal of the wheelbarrow's weight, so ensure the two pieces you use are solid and strong. They should measure 2" to 3" in diameter and be 8" to 12" long.

Building Instructions

STEP **1:** **Assembling the Basic Frame**

This project really starts with the wheel. If you don't have a wheel with a 14-inch diameter, you can still follow the instructions outlined here, but you will have to adjust some of your measurements. The main thing to remember is that the radius of the wheel plus one or two inches will be the height that the handles will be off the ground. (I think it looks better when the wheelbarrow handles are level – it also makes placing flowerpots easier.)

First determine the length of your axle. If you happen to have a wheel with an axle already attached, simply take a measure of the length of the axle. If you only have a wheel, you will obviously need to create an axle of some sort. The simplest way to create an axle is to use a long bolt, secured with a nut. Based on the size of your wheel, get an appropriate sized bolt and note the length.

Get the two pieces you will use as your handles (A). Lay them on your workbench and space them apart in a V-like shape so the axle end is sufficiently wide enough to accommodate the axle, while at the other end the handles are spaced about 33" apart.

The two handles will be joined together using the cross braces (B). The front cross brace needs to be positioned back far enough so as to not interfere with the wheel. It must be at least 10", if not more, away from the axle. The other cross brace should be set about 18" to 24" in from the other end of the handles – the

Figure 1

end that you will ultimately be "handling" to move it around. Cut the pieces to the correct lengths to fit. See Fig. 1.

Because you want to achieve a V-like shape for your handles, the cross braces will not fit really snugly unless they are cut at a bit of an angle. You may also want to create notches in the handles to fit the cross braces and make the joinery that much more secure. If you end up with a snug fit, you can join the cross braces to the handles with screws. If your fit isn't so snug, you would be better off lag bolting the pieces together.

Next, do a test fit of the wheel. If your wheel has an axle, you can determine how to attach it – and the wheel – to what you've assembled so far. For the wheelbarrow pictured on page 111, I simply notched out a groove on the underside of both handles and put on a short metal strip that had predrilled holes in it, then bent it to fit it snugly around the axle. If you are using a bolt for your axle, you will need to drill holes in the handles to accommodate the ends of the axle.

Assuming everything is fitting okay, you can go on to the next step. If not, you have some adjustments to make!

STEP 2: Adding a Basket

To begin assembling the basket, you will need the pieces you are using for the basket uprights (C). The height of the basket will be about 6" to 8" – it shouldn't be much higher, otherwise you won't be able to see much of your flowerpots. Notch and screw each basket upright to the handle and cross brace.

You should have a framework of four uprights. These can now be topped with the rail pieces (D). The two side rails of the basket should be straight. The front and back rails, however, can either be straight or gently curved – your choice. I find the curved pieces look a little nicer. Attach the side pieces first, then the front and back ones. See Fig. 2.

Time to fill in the basket sides (E). Cut the pieces to size to fit the height of your basket. I find that spacing the pieces of wood about 3" apart gives it a good look, but use your discretion. The best way to start is by placing one piece midway between two uprights and then working out in either direction – this saves having to accurately measure them. The side pieces can be screwed in place either to the inside of or underneath the rail, and to the inside or outside of the handle at the bottom.

For a really artistic look, if you have some nice root pieces, you can use them to fill in the basket sides. Use your judgement but make sure they are well secured.

The floor (F) can be made with a few pieces attached to the handles or else some weathered flat pieces. Screw them in place.

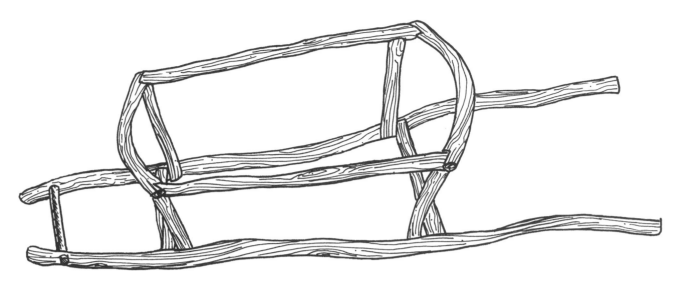

Figure 2

STEP 3: Legs and Bracing

Time to attach the legs (G). Predrill holes and secure the legs to the handle with lag bolts. The legs will also need to be braced. See Fig. 3. The frame should be solid enough, but add more bracing if you feel it's required.

For a finishing touch, I shaped the handles to give the wheelbarrow a comfortable, worn look. You can use a sander or rasp to do so. Finally, attach the wheel in place and you're set to roll your new wheelbarrow around the garden.

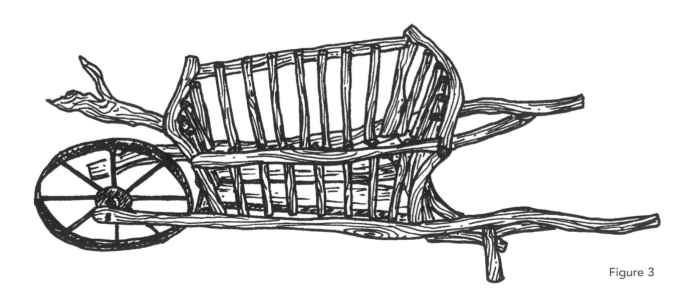

Figure 3

Tricycle

Park me in your garden

MATERIALS

A 1 forked piece, 2" to 3" in diameter, 30" to 36" long

OR 2 curved pieces, 3" to 4" in diameter, 30" to 36" long

B 1 curved piece, 1½" to 2½" in diameter, about 12" long

C 1 curved piece, 2" to 3" in diameter, 30" to 36" long

D 1 straight piece, 2" to 2½" in diameter, 18" long

E 2 curved pieces, 1½" to 2½" in diameter, about 10" to 14" long

F 1 forked piece, 1½" to 2½" in diameter, 8" to 12" long

G 1 curved piece, 1½" to 2" in diameter, 10" to 12" long

H 1 flat piece, 1" to 2" thick, 6" to 8" wide, 10" to 12" long

1 steel rod

1 large wheel

2 small wheels

Assorted screws, lag bolts, nuts and washers, including spring grip washers

Assorted pieces for bracing

TOOLS

Bandsaw/jigsaw

Drill and drill bits

Sanding blocks

Screwdriver

Socket wrench

Choosing Your Wood

Ⓐ Fork

The chances are slim that you'll find a piece of driftwood as I did, which was the inspiration for this entertaining project. It was shaped like the front fork of a bicycle and was hard as a rock. If you have been fortunate enough to find such a piece, great. If not, don't despair, because you can achieve the same look with two curved pieces. See Fig. 1 to get a clear idea of the shape you're looking for.

Ⓑ Handlebars

Although the handlebars can be fashioned out of a slightly curved piece, one with a more exaggerated arc makes for a better look. The size of the piece should be about 12" long and 1½" to 2½" thick.

Ⓒ Main Frame

Search in your driftwood pile for a long, curved piece that will be used as your main frame. The piece should be 2" to 3" in diameter, 30" to 36" in length and have a slight wavy curve, like a stretched out S (also see Fig. 2).

Ⓓ Back Cross Frame

Choose a solid, sturdy piece for the back cross frame that's 2" to 2½" thick and 18" long.

Ⓔ Main Frame Supports

Find two similarly curved pieces for your main frame supports that are 10" to 14" in length and 1½" to 2½" in diameter.

Ⓕ Front Seat Support

Yes, you'll need another forked piece for the front seat support. As it's a smaller piece, though, it's more likely you'll be able to find this kind of piece in your driftwood pile. Look for a piece that's 1½" to 2½" in diameter and 8" to 12" long.

Ⓖ Rear Seat Support

Find a sturdy, curved piece for your rear seat support, ideally 1½" to 2" thick and 10" to 12" long. Remember, a longer piece can always be cut down to suit.

Ⓗ Seat

Keep an eye out for a nicely shaped piece for the seat. It should be 1" to 2" thick, 6" to 8" wide and 10" to 12" long. You may need to shape the right type of piece to get the exact look you want.

Building Instructions

STEP 1: Getting a Handle on It

If you actually managed to find a piece of driftwood correctly shaped for the fork (A), great – you get to

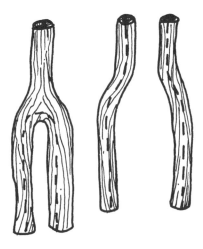

Figure 1

skip a step. If not, you'll need to fashion a fork out of two pieces. Mirror-cut both pieces and screw the flat sides together where they touch each other at the top. See Fig. 1.

Next, get your handlebar piece (B). You'll need to notch it in the middle where it will attach to the top of the fork. Predrill holes in the fork and handlebar and secure together with a lag bolt.

STEP 2: Assembling the Tricycle Frame

Working down the length of the tricycle (see Fig. 2), the next step is to bolt the main frame (C) and the fork together. There is going to be considerable stress where these pieces join, so you'll want to make the fit as snug as you possibly can and use as long a lag bolt as is possible. Predrill holes in the two pieces and connect with the lag bolt.

To attach the back cross frame (D) to what you've assembled so far, you'll have to make a notch near the end of the main frame piece. Predrill holes and secure the two pieces together with a lag bolt.

To finish the tricycle frame, screw the main frame supports (E) to the main frame and back cross frame.

STEP 3: Seat Yourself

To create the seat of the bicycle, it's best to start by screwing the front seat support (F) and rear seat support (G) to the main frame. The forked part of the front seat support should fit around the main frame. If the space between the fork's tines is too small, you will have to trim inside to get a good fit. Screw in place. The

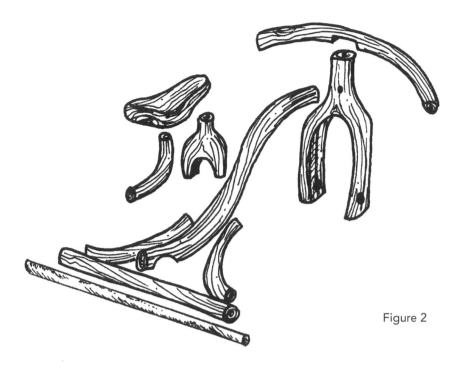

Figure 2

rear seat support is screwed to the main frame at the bottom and to the front seat support at the top. You can now rest the seat piece (H) on top of the two supports and screw it into place.

STEP 4: Attaching the Wheels

Let's start with the wheel at the front of the trike. In order to fit the wheel into the fork I had to trim the insides, but you may be lucky enough not to. Predrill holes near the two ends of the fork for the bolt that will act as the axle. Insert the wheel into the space in the fork and securely bolt it.

As for the rear wheels, mine were salvaged from an old kiddy cart, but any small wheels will do. For the back axle, I used a steel rod that matched the diameter of the holes in the back wheels. These steel rods are readily available at the hardware store. Clamp or strap the axle to the back cross frame, then attach the wheels to the end of the axle and secure with spring grip washers. Your tricycle is now complete.

To create an even more decorative piece, consider adding a flower basket or cart. This is easily done by screwing short lengths of wood together.

Sleigh

Wouldn't Santa be impressed?

MATERIALS

A 1 straight piece with an end curve, 4" to 6" in diameter, 70" to 74" long

B 1 slightly curving piece, 2½" to 3" in diameter, about 28" long

C 1 slightly curving piece, 2½" to 3" in diameter, about 38" long

D 3 straight pieces, 2" to 3" in diameter, about 24" long

E 1 curved piece, 2" to 3" in diameter, about 24" long

F 2 straight pieces, 2" to 3" in diameter, about 45" long

G 2 straight pieces, 2" to 3" in diameter, about 9" long

H 2 straight pieces, 2" to 2½" in diameter, about 24" to 30" long

I 2 straight pieces, 2" to 2½" in diameter, about 19" long

J 1 straight piece, 2" to 2½" in diameter, about 24" to 30" long

K 1 curved piece, 3" to 4" in diameter, about 25" long

L 40 to 60 straight pieces, 1" to 1½" in diameter, about 19" long

OR 20 to 30 straight pieces, 2" to 3" in diameter, about 19" long

M 10 straight to curved pieces, 1½" in diameter, in varying lengths

Assorted pieces for bracing

Assorted screws, nuts, bolts and washers

TOOLS

Bandsaw/jigsaw

Drill and drill bits   Screwdriver

Sander   Socket wrench

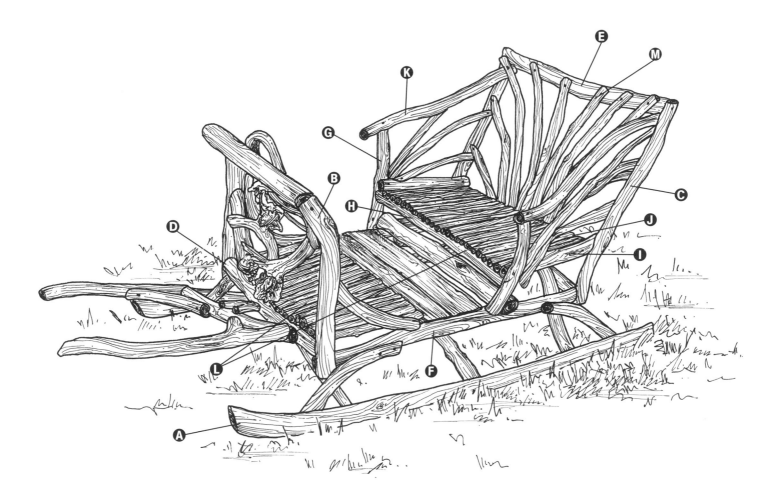

Choosing Your Wood

The sleigh is quite a large project and requires lots of driftwood stock from which to choose your pieces.

Ⓐ Runners

Look in your driftwood pile for a thick piece of driftwood, about 72" long. The piece should be fairly straight, except for the nice curve we need for the front. A tree that has grown out of a steep bank and then grown upwards will give this type of shape. You will end up doing a mirror-image cut to create the two runners – it's hard to have two matching runners without resorting to mirror-cutting.

Ⓑ Front Uprights

Find a slightly curving piece, 2½" to 3" in diameter and about 28"

long. Once cut along its length, you'll get two half-rounds for the front uprights.

Ⓒ Back Uprights

The driftwood needed for the back uprights will be similar to that for the front uprights – slightly curving and 2½" to 3" in diameter – but about 38" long. These will be mirror-cut as well.

Ⓓ Crosspieces

Find three similar pieces in your driftwood pile for the crosspieces. Each one should be reasonably straight, 2" to 3" in diameter and about 24" long.

Ⓔ Back Seat Support

You'll need one nicely curved

piece, 2" to 3" in diameter and about 24" long for the back seat support.

F Stringers

Find two straight pieces, 2" to 3" in diameter and about 45" long for the stringers.

G Arm Uprights

To support the arms, you'll need to find two straight pieces for the uprights, 2" to 3" in diameter and about 9" long.

H Front Seat Rails

You'll want two straight pieces that are 2" to 2½" in diameter and about 24" to 30" long for the front seat rails. Keep an eye out for a similar piece for the rear seat rail.

I Side Seat Rails

Once again, you'll need two straight pieces, 2" to 2½" in diameter, this time about 19" long.

J Rear Seat Rail

Perhaps you've already set this piece aside from an earlier search. If not, go find a straight piece, 2" to 2½" in diameter and about 24" to 30" long.

K Arms

Although it would be nice to find two matching pieces, due to the unique curve needed for the arms, a single nicely shaped piece can be mirror-cut to get the symmetry we're looking for. Find a piece that's 3" to 3½" in diameter and about 25" long from end to end.

L Floor and Seat

Depending on the size of the pieces you're using, you'll need about 40 to 60 straight pieces, 1" to 1½" in diameter, each about 19" long for the floor and seat of the sleigh. If you're really stretching your driftwood pile, though, and don't mind the extra work, you may want to use 20 to 30 straight pieces that are 2" to 3" in diameter, again about 19" long, and mirror-cut them to double the quantity. Just be careful they don't warp.

M Back

The best pieces for the back are those that you just haven't been able to use in other projects because they are too kinked, too oddly curved or too short. You'll need about 10 pieces, but you may want to pick out about a half dozen more, then decide exactly which pieces you want to use once the seat is already built.

Building Instructions

I hope you will have built some of the other pieces by now before tackling the sleigh. It's not that it is more difficult, but it does incorporate many of the more important aspects of the previous creations (i.e., mirror-cutting, intense bracing and following an orderly assembly).

STEP **1**: **Starting from the Ground Up**

We start with the runners (A). I found a nice piece for my runners. Because it was reasonably thick, I chose to mirror-cut it down the middle to create two matching pieces. Unless you are lucky enough to find two similar pieces for the two runners, you'll have to do the same. Be careful your pieces don't warp after cutting. If they do, you'll just have to set them aside to use on some other project.

Take your front and back uprights (B and C) and cut them lengthwise to create two sets of matching pieces. Isn't mirror-cutting wonderful? Now take one of the runners and find its centerpoint. The two uprights will be 45" apart, roughly centered to the runner, so measure 22½" from that centerpoint in each direction and predrill holes for the bolts. Do the same with the other runner, and predrill holes in the uprights as well. Then fasten the uprights to the runners with nuts, bolts and washers. This is one of the few times I suggest that you use them, but since these are very crucial joints, I recommend you do so.

STEP 2: The Main Frame

Get the pieces you're using for the crosspieces (D) and the back seat support (E). Two of the crosspieces will be affixed 9" up from the runner, one at the front, one at the back. The third crosspiece is attached at the top of the two front uprights and the back seat support will be attached at the top of the two back uprights. Predrill holes, then fasten with lag bolts. Don't skimp on the length of these lag bolts. After all, this is your main frame.

Next come the stringers (F) that complete the "floor" of the sleigh. Again, predrill and then lag bolt these to the four uprights. You can always have the stringers rest on the crosspieces at the front and back. If you do so, then I'd recommend you notch the stringers for extra support.

STEP 3: Finishing the Frame

It's now time to attach the two arm uprights (G). These will be bolted against the arms and stringers. Notch where they touch the stringers and cut a flat spot where you will attach them to the flat surface of the arms. Predrill and bolt together.

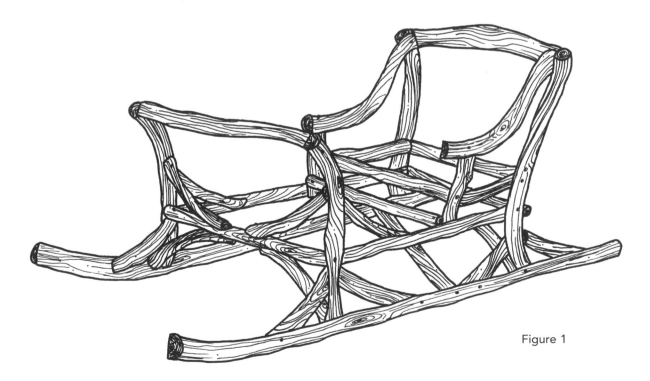

Figure 1

A Horse-Drawn Sleigh

If you're planning to hook a wicker horse or reindeer to your sleigh, you'll want to construct the following piece.

You'll need:
- **a** 2 straight pieces, 2½" to 3" in diameter, about 62" long
- **b** 1 straight piece, 3" in diameter, about 22" long
- **c** 2 curved pieces, 2" to 3" in diameter, for bracing

Assorted screws and bolts

A long piece of leather or twine

You'll be assembling the pieces as per the sketch below. Pre-drill holes into the two long pieces (a) and the short, straight piece (b), then screw together. Attach the bracing pieces (c).

Next, bolt the short, straight piece to the frame of the sleigh. Finally, make a loop out of your piece of leather, twine or cord and lay it over your wicker reindeer or horse. Slip the long pieces into each end of the loop and there you have it – a horse/reindeer-drawn sleigh.

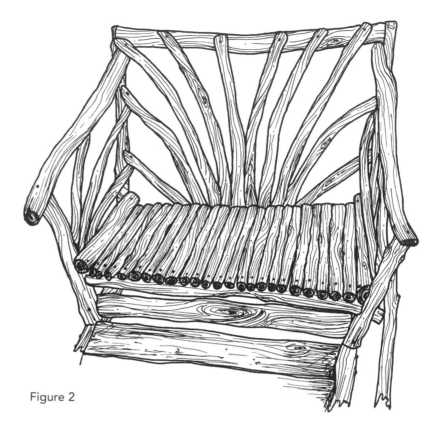

Figure 2

Next, you will bolt the front seat rails (H) in position, as in Fig. 1. Do the same for the side seat rails (I) and rear seat rail (J). The last parts of the basic frame are the arms (K). Be sure to use lag bolts for these.

Now your basic frame is finished. Stand back and take a good overall look. Does it look right? Are the runners facing the right way? Just checking….

Next, you will want to brace the sleigh. Bracing is very important for this structure. Look at Fig. 1 for guidance. Don't be afraid of overdoing it – too much bracing is better than too little.

STEP 4: Floor, Seat and Back

Once you feel satisfied that your creation is solid, you can begin laying the floor and seat pieces (L). If you are using round pieces, look at your pile of 40 to 60 pieces and sort them by diameter. Keep those about 1" thick in one pile, and those closer to 1½" thick in another. That way you

can use one pile for the floor pieces and the other for the seat pieces – thus each area is roughly even-looking.

If you are only using 20 to 30 pieces, you can sort them by size as well. Then, if you haven't undertaken the task of cutting them lengthwise, there's no time like the present to do so. They will be placed flat side down on the seat and floor.

Whichever type of pieces you end up using, your next job is to screw all the pieces in place.

Finally, decide on your design for the back seat. Determine how you'll lay out the back pieces (M), or follow my sketch (see Fig. 2) and then screw them in place.

Congratulations! You've finished the sleigh. The front can be gussied up with rootwood, deer horns, bells, and so on. I made the one in the photograph for my neighbors, and they filled it with colored parcels and strung up lights on it for Christmas. Complete with a full-size wicker reindeer, it made a pretty picture indeed.

Hanging Flowerbox

A nice, easy project to begin your driftwood adventure

MATERIALS

A 1 straight piece, 2½" to 3" in diameter, 24" long

B 2 straight pieces, 2" to 3" in diameter, 24" long

C 1 curved piece, 2" to 3" in diameter, 24" long

D 8 straight pieces, 2" to 3" in diameter, 6" long

E 2 straight pieces, 2" to 3" in diameter, 9" long

F 6 straight pieces, 2" to 3" in diameter, 6" long

G 4 straight pieces, 2" to 3" in diameter, cut to fit

H 1 curved piece, 2" to 3" in diameter, 24" to 28" long

I 2 straight pieces, 2" to 3" in diameter, 9" to 12" long

J 7 straight pieces, 2" to 3" in diameter, cut to fit

Assorted small pieces for bracing

Assorted screws

TOOLS

Bandsaw/jigsaw

Drill and drill bits   Screwdriver

Choosing Your Wood

Ⓐ Main Wall Supports

For these support pieces, you will want to search in your driftwood pile for a length of sturdy, well-seasoned wood. It should be about 2½" to 3" in diameter and 24" long. By cutting it in half lengthwise, you'll have two pieces for your supports.

Ⓑ Secondary Wall Supports

Find two nice, straight lengths, each 24" long.

Ⓒ Front rail

A nicely curved piece of driftwood, 24" long, is needed for the front rail.

Ⓓ Front Rungs

Eight pieces, about 6" long each, are used for the rungs. Short pieces are often in abundance when you search your driftwood reserves. If not, longer pieces can be cut down to create the individual 6" lengths.

Ⓔ Side Rails

Unlike the front rail, the side rails are straight, so you'll need to find two straight pieces that are 2" to 3" in diameter and 9" long.

Ⓕ Side Rungs

Similar to the front rungs, you'll need short pieces for the side

Note: I made this unit to accommodate three 6"-diameter flowerpots. Once you've had the experience of building this one, you can try your hand at customizing the design to build to whatever size you want.

rungs – in total, six straight pieces that are 2" to 3" in diameter and 6" long.

Ⓖ Bottom

You will need four straight pieces, about 2" to 3" in diameter for the bottom of the flower box, but the length of them will be determined by how much curve there is in your front rail. When choosing the pieces, keep in mind that you will be cutting each one into half-rounds to create eight pieces in total.

Ⓗ Roof Rail

Look for a curved piece similar to the front rail, slightly longer if you prefer (24" to 28").

Ⓘ Roof Side Rails

Two strong, straight pieces between 9" and 12" long are needed as sturdy side rails to support the roof.

Ⓙ Roof Beams

You'll need about seven straight pieces for the roof beams. Due to the curve of the roof rail, each beam will have to be cut to fit, but each piece should still be about 2" to 3" in diameter. Again, keep in mind that each of these pieces will be cut in half lengthwise to create half-rounds.

Building Instructions

STEP 1: Constructing the Wall Support

Take the 24" piece you've chosen for your main wall support (A) and mirror-cut it to create two half-round pieces. You don't want this piece to warp because it will be your main

support that will be screwed flat to a wall or the side of your shed – wherever it is you'll be mounting your hanging flowerbox. If the pieces do warp, then set them aside to use on some other project, and have another try.

Take the two secondary wall support pieces (B) and make round notches in each end. Attach the notched pieces to the half-rounds and secure with screws. See Fig. 1.

Figure 1

STEP 2: Building the Box

Take your front rail piece (C) and mirror-cut this down its length to give yourself a matching top and bottom rail. Get the eight 6" pieces you'll use for your front rungs (D) and line them up along the rails to get a sense of spacing. Screw them

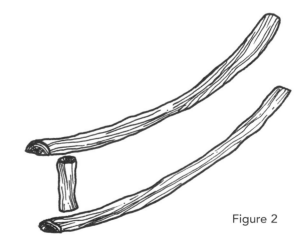

Figure 2

TIP To give me more purchase on the screws, I screwed them through the back of the frame on an angle.

in evenly between the two rails. See Fig. 2. If, by chance, the rails warped a little, then slice some of the rail sufficiently to allow the rungs to be attached evenly.

To join the front rail to the frame, take the two side rail pieces (E) and make two mirror cuts, so you have a total of four 9"-long pieces. Predrill holes into the constructed wall support and the front rail and screw the side rail into them. See Fig. 3. To install the side rungs (F), leave them round and screw in three pieces per side to the flat surface of the side rails.

For the floor of the box, I took my four bottom pieces (G), cut them down the middle and laid the flat side down on the front of the bottom rail in between each rung and screwed them in position. See Fig. 4. The back was screwed down on the back frame. This should give sufficient strength to support your flower pots.

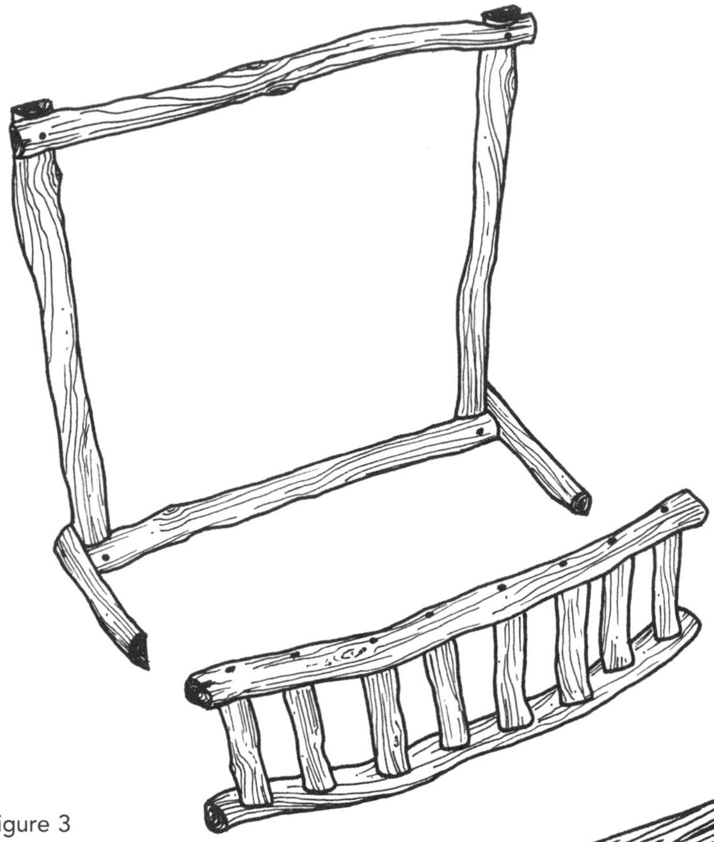

Figure 3

Figure 4

STEP 3: Raising the Roof

To attach your roof rail piece (H) to the top frame, screw the two side rails (I) to the roof rail piece first, then affix the whole assembly to the frame. Add two braces to strengthen the roof structure.

Cut the roof beams (J) into mirror images and place them so they touch each other at the back and splay out about 2" apart at the ends. See Fig. 5.

Measure and fit each piece individually. I did try to space them evenly apart, but the effect was not as nice.

STEP 4: Flower Up

Finally, you can screw the whole constructed piece to the wall with at least four screws. If you think it needs more support for the flowers, then just install a brace or two under the rail and to the wall. You're done. Now all it needs is flowers.

TIP If you make the roof beams overhang the roof support about 2" you'll create a nice canopy effect.

Figure 5

Wine Rack

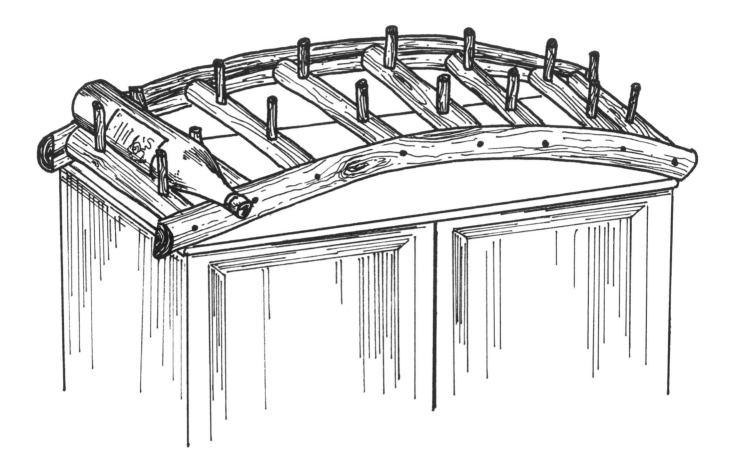

A good gift project for the driftwood novice

MATERIALS		TOOLS
A 1 curved piece, 2" to 2½" in diameter, 24" to 30" long OR 2 similarly curved pieces, about 2" in diameter, 24" to 30" long **B** 8 straight pieces, 1" to 2½" in diameter, 9" long	**C** 16 straight pieces, ¼" to ½" thick, 4" long #8 screws Wood glue	Bandsaw Drill and drill bits Drill press (optional) Sander/sanding block Screwdriver

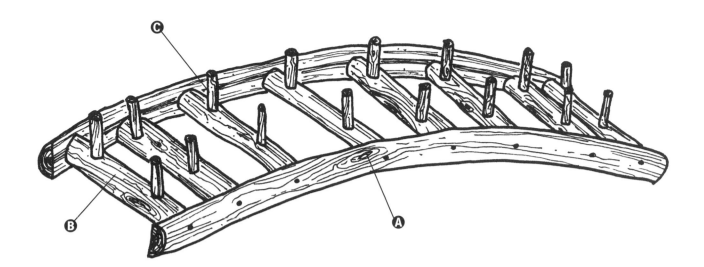

Choosing Your Wood

Ⓐ Main Frame

If you have a nice and hard curved piece, 2" to 2½" thick and 24" to 30" long, you can cut it in half lengthwise (mirror-cut it). This will give you a flat inside surface that is easier to attach the crossbars to. You can use two similarly curved pieces instead, but then the crossbars will need notching on both ends to fit snugly against the two curves.

Ⓑ Crossbars

You shouldn't have too much trouble finding a couple of straight lengths from which to cut your eight or so crossbars.

Ⓒ Pegs

Another easy group to find are the roughly sixteen pegs. If you have any uniquely shaped pieces, you could install a few of them to add to the character of the wine rack – perhaps one on each end.

Building Instructions

If you are using one piece for the main frame (A), mirror-cut it using your bandsaw. The crossbars (B) will need to be identical in length – if they aren't already, cut each piece to the appropriate 9" length.

You'll need to drill two holes in each crossbar, 1" in from each end and ½" deep. This is easiest accomplished with a drill press. If you don't have one, try to use someone's for the day to save yourself a hassle. Fit and glue each peg (C) in the holes of the crossbars.

Now you can begin predrilling and screwing the crossbars to the main frame. If you are using two round pieces for the frame, you'll need to notch both ends of each crossbar (as mentioned above) before screwing them to the frame.

To space the crossbars appropriately, ensure the pegs are 3¼" apart at their base. Use #8 screws. If, as you move along the length of the frame, you are keeping the distance at a consistent 3¼", there should be no problem of anything becoming crooked.

Arbor

A distinct highlight in your garden

MATERIALS

A 4 straight pieces, 2" to 3" in diameter, 6½' to 7' long

B 2 straight pieces, 2" to 3" in diameter, 6½' to 7' long

C 2 curved pieces, 2" to 3" in diameter, 6½' to 7' long

   OR 1 curved piece, 3" to 5" in diameter, 6½' to 7' long

   OR 4 curved pieces, 2" to 3" in diameter, about 3½' long

D 2 straight pieces, 2" to 3" in diameter, 5' long

E 4 straight pieces, 2" in diameter, 4' long

F 20 to 40 randomly shaped pieces, 1" to 1½" in diameter, varied lengths

Small curved pieces for bracing

Assorted screws and lag bolts

Cement blocks or flat stones

Steel rods

Decorative pieces (optional)

TOOLS

Bandsaw/jigsaw   Screwdriver

Drill and drill bits   Socket wrench

Sander

Choosing Your Wood

Ⓐ Base Supports

You'll need a total of four fairly straight lengths of wood, 2" to 3" in diameter and 6½' to 7' long. These are going to be the main supports for your arbor, so ensure they are solid and strong pieces.

Ⓑ Caps

Find some more long pieces in your wood pile for the cap – about 6½' to 7' in length and 2" to 3" thick.

Ⓒ Arches

Ideally, for the best support, you should find two curved pieces for the arches, each 6½' to 7' in length and 2" to 3" thick. However, you can always make do with one piece by mirror-cutting it. It should still be a 6½' to 7' long piece, but thicker – from 3" to 5" in diameter. If your stock of wood just won't allow for either of these options, you can also use four shorter, curved pieces, 2" to 3" in diameter, and each about 3½' long.

D Upper Crosspieces

Use two straight, solid pieces for the upper crosspieces. They should be about 2" to 3" in diameter – about the same thickness as the base supports and caps – but only about 5' long.

E Lower Crosspieces

These four pieces need to be about 2" thick and 4' long.

F Side and Roof Pieces

Pull out 20 to 40 pieces in a variety of shapes – curved, Y-shaped, L-shaped, etc. (You are better off saving your good, straight pieces for another project). Look for pieces that are about 1" to 1½" thick in a variety of lengths.

Figure 1

Building Instructions

STEP **1**: Creating the Trellis Frame

To start building the trellis, you'll need to gather your base supports (A) and caps (B). Start with a pair of base supports and one cap piece – you will be assembling one side of the frame first, then the other. Top the two base supports with the cap piece. Keep in mind that the caps should overhang the edges by about 12" on each side. See Fig. 1. Notch the cap piece, predrill holes, then lag bolt to the base supports. Repeat these steps for the other cap piece and pair of base supports.

Next, add the arches (C). Your assembly will be slightly different depending on the quantity and shape of the wood you're using. If you were able to collect two pieces, simply notch and lag bolt each one to each side of the frame, as in Fig. 1.

If you have only one piece to use for the arches, you will need to mirror-cut it first, before notching and lag bolting the pieces to the two sides of the frame. Hopefully this piece doesn't warp. If it does, you will have to set it aside for another project and collect some more wood.

Finally, if you've elected to use four pieces of wood, you'll need to create the two arches first. You may want to attach these arch pieces to a secondary cap piece, rather than the cap (A). Whether or not you decide to do this will depend on the shape of your cap and the kind of look you want to achieve. See the illustration on page 133 for one example of how I did it.

Now it's time to connect the two sides of the frame. As with the caps, you may want the upper crosspieces (D) to have some overhang. I find it looks good if it's projected about 12" to 18" on each side. Attach the upper crosspieces to your pair of frames by notching and lag bolting all joints. This will give you a nice, solid structure. Then, for support at the bottom of the arbor, add the lower crosspieces (E). Once again, predrill and lag bolt them in place. See Fig. 2.

Now that your basic frame is assembled, put it on a level surface and check for stability. There are still pieces to be added, so it likely won't be rock solid, but it shouldn't wobble around. If it does, you may need to trim one or more of the legs to get everything level.

Figure 2

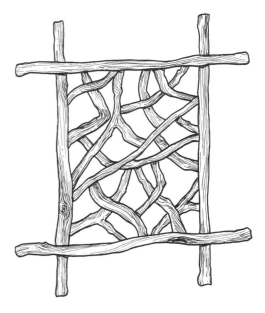

Figure 3

STEP 2: Sides, Roof and Bracing

This is where your creativity can really take off. As you can see in Fig. 3, there are a variety of looks you can go for. Follow any one of my designs or just randomly join side and roof pieces (F) together. Remember, the more pieces you use in the roof, the shadier your arbor will be. You can finish stabilizing the arbor by bracing all the overhangs with nice, curved pieces, if you have them. Try rocking the structure a little. If it needs more bracing, add some more pieces, but don't spoil the lines of your project in the process. Always stand back and give it a good once-over to see if it looks well-balanced.

When you determine where you would like to place your arbor, be sure to put flat stones or cement blocks under all four legs to protect it from damage. Then anchor the arbor to the ground by driving two steel rods into the ground beside at least two of the legs and securing the legs to the rods.

Boat

An attention-getter beyond words

MATERIALS

A 2 curved pieces, 2" to 2½" in diameter, 78" long

B 2 slightly curved pieces, 2" to 2½" in diameter, about 68" long

C 1 curved piece, 2½" to 3" in diameter, 28" long

D 1 straight piece, 1½" to 2" in diameter, about 36" long

E 18 to 20 straight pieces, 1" to 2" in diameter, varied lengths up to 28"

F 9 to 10 straight pieces, 1" to 2" in diameter, cut to fit

G 20 to 40 straight to curved pieces, 1" to 1½" in diameter, varied lengths OR other materials

H 1 straight piece, 2" to 4" in diameter, 5' to 6' long

I Assorted pieces, planking or crating

J 20 to 30 pieces, 1½" to 2" in diameter, varied lengths

OR assorted pieces of crating

K 1 straight piece, 1½" to 2½" in diameter, 66" long

L 5 curved pieces, 1½" to 2½" in diameter, varied lengths

Assorted screws, lag bolts, hooks and screw eyes

Assorted pieces for bracing

TOOLS

Bandsaw/jigsaw

Clamps

Drill and drill bits

Sander

Screwdriver

Socket wrench

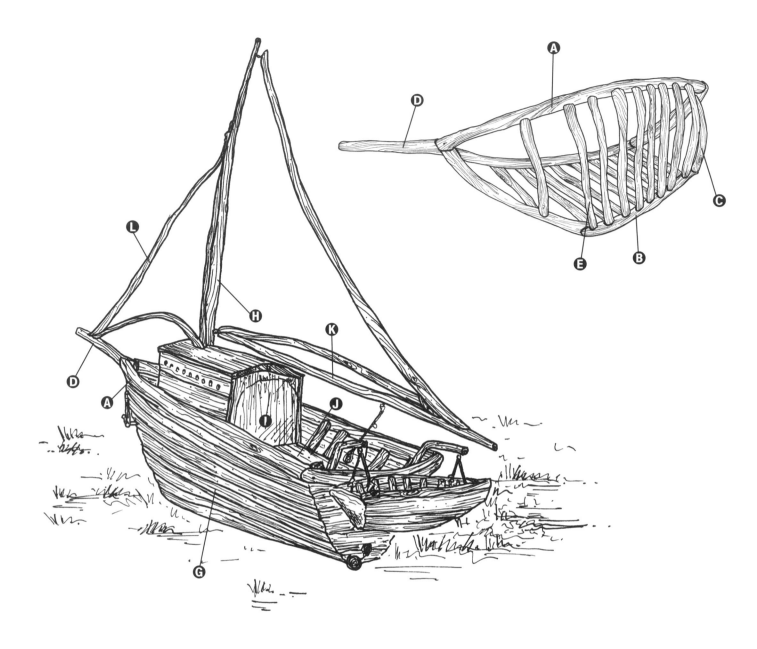

Choosing Your Wood

This is one of those projects that requires a large assortment of curved pieces from which to choose.

Ⓐ Gunwales

The gunwales are best made from two pieces that closely match each other in curvature. If in dire straits, you could do a mirror-cut, but there is a danger of warping that would likely ruin the piece. So try to find that elusive pair! What you're looking for are two curved pieces that are 2" to 2½" thick and 78" in length.

Ⓑ Keel

It's quite unlikely that you'll be able to find a single properly shaped piece for the keel. If you are fortunate enough to do so, great. Most likely, though, you'll need to find two slightly curved pieces, as I did, that are 2" to 2½" in diameter and approximately 68" long, that will be attached together during the boat assembly.

☉ Stern Supports

One curved piece of driftwood that's 2½" to 3" in diameter and about 20" long will suffice for the stern supports, as you'll do a mirror-cut to produce the two pieces that are required.

☉ Bowsprit

Find a nice, straight piece for the bowsprit. It should be about 36" long and 1½" to 2" thick.

☉ Ribs

Sift through your driftwood pile for 18 to 20 reasonably straight pieces. These should be of substantial thickness, about 1" to 2" in diameter; the lengths you'll need will vary. Try to find pieces that are 26" to 28" long – you can always cut them to fit later.

☉ Deck Supports (not visible)

Look for similar pieces as you did for the ribs, about 1" to 2" in diameter. For now, just find pieces that range from 20" to 30". Grab a few extras just in case. You'll definitely have to cut at least some of them to get the right fit.

☉ Planking

You have some choice in your planking materials. You can either find about 20 to 40 driftwood pieces, varied in length and degree of curvature, that are 1" to 1½" in diameter; or you can substitute driftwood with another material that will give the boat a good look. It's up to you.

☉ Mast

Find a strong, solid and straight piece of driftwood for the mast. It'll need to be 5' to 6' in length and anywhere from 2" to 4" thick.

☉ Wheelhouse

If you have driftwood planking material, great. Old crating, however, acts as a good substitute, especially if it's nicely weathered.

☉ Decking

Your decking materials can either be driftwood or weathered crating. You'll need 20 to 30 pieces of driftwood, but 40 to 60 pieces of crating, depending on size.

☉ Boom

Check your woodpile for a nice, straight boom piece. It'll need to be 66" long and about 1½" to 2½" in diameter.

☉ Sail

Find five nicely curved pieces for the sail. The illustration on the opposite page will give you an idea of the kind of shapes you're looking for. The lengths of each piece will vary, so you may want to find some extra-long pieces that you're prepared to cut down to size.

Building Instructions

Without a doubt, this is a big project but, oh! – what a unique garden sculpture. It will be a lot of work, rest assured, but don't let this deter you from tackling the project because it will give you a sense of satisfaction like no other.

STEP 1: Assembling the Main Boat Frame

As you can see in Fig. 1, the boat is constructed upside down (at least in the first stages). A picnic table makes for a good place to build the frame.

to fit each other (see Fig. 2) and then screw them together.

Mirror-cut the piece for the stern supports (C). Predrill holes, then attach both pieces to the gunwales, using lag bolts. Once this is done, you can bolt the assembled keel to the stern supports and gunwales.

Finally, the bowsprit (D) will need to be shaped before it can be attached to the rest of the frame. It should be flattened at the back, or stern, end with a bandsaw so it will fit flush with the gunwales. Predrill holes and use a lag bolt to attach the bowsprit to the frame.

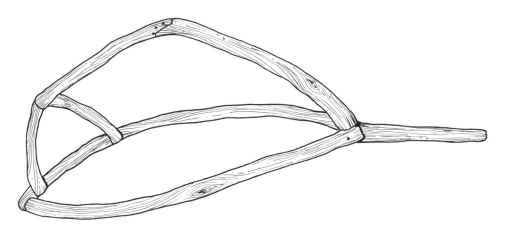

Figure 1

You'll be assembling the frame as shown in Fig. 1. Predrill holes in the two gunwale pieces (A) and connect together with lag bolts. To create the keel (B) out of your two pieces of driftwood, you'll need to cut the two

STEP 2: Attaching the Ribs and Planking

Gather together your bundle of ribs (E). You'll likely need about 9 to 10 per side. Each rib will be screwed to a

Figure 2

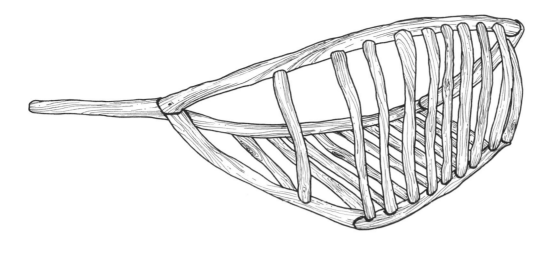

Figure 3

gunwale at one end and the keel at the other. You may need to cut some pieces to ensure a good fit. See Fig. 3. If you can keep the ribs in reasonable alignment, it will make the planking easier.

Install the deck supports (F) next. These will be screwed onto the ribs across the width of the boat about 5" from the gunwales. You will have to do some cutting to get the right fit. See Fig. 4.

As mentioned earlier, you have some choices to make for the planking (G). If you would like to keep the project a purely driftwood undertaking, you'll need to have 20 to 40 pieces of wood on hand and split them in two to create the planks. You can also use "artistic license" as I did. I happened upon some 50-year-old crating outside a factory, and it made for perfect planking material because the patina matched the rest of the wood I was using.

Start planking on the keel and screw each piece to the ribs, lapping each layer as you work your way up the sides. Cut all pieces to butt at the ribs.

STEP 3: Mast, Wheelhouse and Deck

If you haven't done so already, you can now turn the boat over and proceed with construction of the mast and deck.

Find the piece you've chosen for your mast (H). It will be attached to the keel by bolting with a lag bolt from underneath. You'll also need to screw the mast to one of the deck supports. Plus, for extra stability, jam a bracer between the mast and the next deck support. See Fig. 5. Screw the bracer piece in place.

Construct a frame for the wheelhouse to your own idea of the right shape. Screw onto the deck around the mast. Add planking on all sides. By drilling some 1" holes, you can create portholes.

If you are using planks for your decking, lay them lengthwise and screw to the decking. The same can be done with mirror-cut driftwood pieces – just ensure the flat sides are lying face-up.

Figure 4

STEP 4: Sail Away

On to the sail. Find your boom and sail pieces (K and L). You may need to cut these down to size. I bolted the three front sail pieces to the bowsprit and mast. For the rear sail, I used a hook and screw eye to attach the boom to the mast. I did the same for the rear sail, then bolted it to the boom for stability. The final sail piece was screwed to the rear sail and boom. See the photo on page 137.

Finishing touches are up to you. I had a stroke of luck when I found a brass candleholder with a propeller base at a sidewalk sale. Once unscrewed, I had a nice ship bell and propeller. My wheel was made from a brass cogged gear that I had in a box of odds and ends. Once buffed up, it looked great. What you end up with depends on what you have and what you can find. See what you can scrounge up.

If you want to add a little lifeboat, as I did, the process is easy. Basically, you will need to follow the first few steps of this project all over again, just on a smaller scale. Or, if you have a junior assistant on hand, he or she can build this little piece while you're tackling the larger one.

As a final touch, you may want to add lights all around the outline. I'd recommend doing so. It really highlights this driftwood masterpiece.

Figure 5

Conclusion

The last five years have been quite a learning experience. Making garden furniture from driftwood came to me as easy as falling off a log, as they say. Creating this book was a greater challenge.

My four children, after they learned that I had grandiose ideas about writing a book, insisted I invest in a computer. I felt that perhaps they were right and thereby started my first learning curve. There were many others that plunged me into the quagmire of the modern recording and communications world.

My grandchildren take this all for granted. To me, however, CD burners, high-speed modems, Internet hookups, software that challenges your sanity and digital cameras are things that leave me staring at my monitor with a blank expression on my face and my pupils reduced to tiny dots.

I don't know where I am, or how I got there, or what happened to my stuff that I just typed or that picture that I saved, but now the Finder won't even tell me where the computer's hidden it. Whatever happened to the Gestetner stencil duplicator? Go on, tell me you've never heard of it – wallow in your ignorance. Go ask your grandmother. She probably used one at school.

All kidding aside, after the growing pains were gone, I came to love this new technology. When my publisher, Lionel Koffler, first said to me that the distance between me and Firefly Books was not a problem, I had my doubts. Nevertheless, he was right. By using the Internet, fax machines, telephones and couriers, I communicated everything the publisher needed without venturing out on any highway.

Why did I come to write this book? Two reasons: one, imagination, and two, lack of energy. After discovering this latent talent of combining my imagination with some woodworking skill, I found that I could make items that appealed to others. A lot of people were asking if I sold this "stuff." I have sold a few pieces, but the energy required to go and collect at the beach and then build the items was just too much for me.

Then one day at a mall that was kindly displaying my "stuff," a man was standing there looking at the items. He said, "You know, I'm a carpenter and I can follow any plans, but I wouldn't know where to start with these." The idea was sown right then. I'll tell people how to make items and they can go and get their own driftwood.

I believe that everyone likes to leave a footprint or two in this world before they leave. I hope you have enjoyed a few of mine and that some of you will follow in them. Mother Nature would like that too.

Index